BARRON'S

EARLY ACHIEVER

GRADE 1

ENGLISH LANGUAGE ARTS WORKBOOK

ACTIVITIES & PRACTICE

REVIEW · UNDERSTAND · DISCOVER

T0016067

Copyright © 2022 by Kaplan North America, LLC, d/b/a Barron's Educational Series

Previously published under the title *Barron's Common Core Success Grade 1 English Language Arts* by Kaplan North America, LLC, d/b/a Barron's Educational Series

All rights reserved.
No part of this publication may be reproduced in any form, or
by any means without the written permission of the copyright owner.

Published by Kaplan North America, LLC, d/b/a Barron's Educational Series
1515 W. Cypress Creek Road
Fort Lauderdale, FL 33309
www.barronseduc.com

ISBN 978-1-5062-8134-6

10 9 8 7 6 5 4 3 2 1

Kaplan North America, LLC, d/b/a Barron's Educational Series print books are available at special quantity discounts to use for sales promotions, employee premiums, or educational purposes. For more information or to purchase books, please call the Simon & Schuster special sales department at 866-506-1949.

Photo Credits: Title page ©Blend Images/Shutterstock, Page x and x.i ©Matthew Cole/Shutterstock, Page 2 ©Sergey Novikov/Shutterstock, Page 5 ©Teguh Mujiono/Shutterstock (frog); ©Mr.Nikon/Shutterstock (lily pad), Page 6 ©michaeljung/Shutterstock, Page 7 ©Marta Tobolova/Shutterstock, Page 9 ©racorn/Shutterstock, Page 10 ©Blend Images/Shutterstock, Page 15 ©PinkyWinky/Shutterstock, Page 18 ©Goodluz/Shutterstock, Page 25 ©Darrin Henry/Shutterstock, Page 26 ©Oksana Kuzmina/Shutterstock, Page 34 ©mhatzapa/Shutterstock, Page 35 ©BlueRingMedia/Shutterstock, Page 36 ©Vova Shevchuk/Shutterstock (pin on map); ©Syda Productions/Shutterstock (girl), Page 37 ©hircus/Shutterstock, Page 38 XiXinXing/Shutterstock, Page 39 ©Alena Salanovich/Shutterstock (city map); ©hircus/Shutterstock (compass rose), Page 40 ©Hurst Photo/Shutterstock, Page 41 ©Godruma/Shutterstock, Page 45 ©natrot/Shutterstock (notepad), Page 48 ©Novikov Alex/Shutterstock, Page 49 ©WitthayaP/Shutterstock, Page 50 ©Schalke fotografie/Melissa Schalke/Shutterstock, Page 52 ©Willyam Bradberry/Shutterstock, Page 55 ©ArchMan/Shutterstock (dolphin), Page 57 ©Attitude/Shutterstock (background); ©Mikhail Kolesnikov/Shutterstock (trunk); ©89studio/Shutterstock (paper), Page 58 ©Villiers Steyn/Shutterstock, Page 59 ©Natalia Deriabina/Shutterstock (photo); ©ducu59us/Shutterstock (map), Page 60 ©Abstract Design Element/Shutterstock, Page 61 ©Patryk Kosmider/Shutterstock (elephant); ©WitthayaP/Shutterstock (dolphin); ©tachyglossus/Shutterstock (waves), Page 62 ©Steve Bower/Shutterstock (elephant); ©Willyam Bradberry/Shutterstock (dolphin), Page 65 ©Vectors.1/Shutterstock (block); ©Fetullah Mercan/Shutterstock (soccerball); ©Schalke fotografie/Melissa Schalke/Shutterstock, (dolphin), Page 66 ©Schalke fotografie | Melissa Schalke/Shutterstock, Page 67 ©Andrei Shumskiy/Shutterstock, Page 69 ©Blackspring/Shutterstock, Page 70 ©tanoochai/Shutterstock, Page 74 ©Angela Waye/Shutterstock, Page 78 ©CREATISTA/Shutterstock, Page 79 ©lavitrei/Shutterstock, Page 80 ©sbego/Shutterstock, Page 81 ©sbego/Shutterstock, Page 82 ©Regissercom/Shutterstock (all images), Page 83 ©sbego/Shutterstock (hair, door); ©Tanya K/Shutterstock (spoon); ©Lack-O'Keen/Shutterstock (happy face), Page 84 ©Banzainer/Shutterstock (all), Page 85 ©Matthew Cole/Shutterstock, Page 86 ©Arkela/Shutterstock (broken chair); ©sbego/Shutterstock (girl, bears); ©Banzainer/Shutterstock (fox), Page 87 ©Banzainer/Shutterstock (fox); ©sbego/Shutterstock (bear), Page 91 ©frnsys/Shutterstock, Page 92 ©Diana Hlevnjak/Shutterstock, Page 93 ©Yulia-Bogdanova/Shutterstock (background); ©panki/Shutterstock (sparrow), Page 96 ©Boykung/Shutterstock, Page 102 ©NEILRAS/Shutterstock (scene); ©Margo Sokolovskaya/Shutterstock (girl), Page 103 ©Jon Bilous/Shutterstock, Page 106 ©Serega K Photo and Video/Shutterstock, Page 107 ©Gruffi/Shutterstock (book) ©Jon Bilous/Shutterstock (scene); Page 109 ©AlexKaplun/Shutterstock (tree); ©Mad Dog/Shutterstock (sun); ©Matthew Cole/Shutterstock (grass, sleeping); ©Lizavetka/Shutterstock (dog), Page 115 ©Vectomart/Shutterstock (background); ©Natalia Skripko/Shutterstock (pig); ©Jane Kelly/Shutterstock (camel), Page 119 ©Kazakova Maryia/Shutterstock (farm); ©Jaimie Duplass/Shutterstock (girl), Page 120 ©Volosina/Shutterstock (wheat); ©Perutskyi Petro/Shutterstock (seed), Page 121 ©Joe Gough/Shutterstock, Page 123 ©Tatiana Ciumac/Shutterstock, Page 126–127 ©natrot/Shutterstock

Introduction

Barron's Early Achiever workbooks are based on sound educational practices and include both parent-friendly and teacher-friendly explanations of specific learning goals and how students can achieve them through fun and interesting activities and practice. This exciting series mirrors the way English Language Arts is taught in the classroom. Early Achiever Grade 1 English Language Arts presents these skills through different units of related materials that reinforce each learning goal in a meaningful way. The Review, Understand, and Discover sections assist parents, teachers, and tutors in helping students apply skills at a higher level. Additionally, students will become familiar and comfortable with the manner of presentation and learning, as this is what they experience every day in the classroom. These factors will help early achievers master the skills and learning goals in English Language Arts and will also provide an opportunity for parents to play a larger role in their children's education.

Learning Goals for English Language Arts

The following explanation of educational goals is based on what your child will learn in first grade.

Reading Foundational Skills

Phonological Awareness

- Distinguish long from short vowel sounds in spoken single-syllable words.
- Orally produce single-syllable words by blending sounds (phonemes), including consonant blends.
- Isolate and pronounce initial, medial vowel, and final sounds (phonemes) in spoken single-syllable words.
- Segment spoken single-syllable words into their complete sequence of individual sounds (phonemes).

Phonics and Word Recognition

- Know the spelling-sound correspondences for common consonant digraphs.
- Decode regularly spelled one-syllable words.
- Know final –e and common vowel team conventions for representing long vowel sounds.

- Use knowledge that every syllable must have a vowel sound to determine the number of syllables in a printed word.
- Decode two-syllable words following basic patterns by breaking the words into syllables.
- Read words with inflectional endings.
- Recognize and read grade-appropriate irregularly spelled words.

Fluency

- Read grade-level text with purpose and understanding.
- Read grade-level text orally with accuracy, appropriate rate, and expression on successive readings.
- Use context to confirm or self-correct word recognition and understanding, rereading as necessary.

Reading Comprehension Skills

Key Ideas and Details

- Ask and answer questions about key details in a text.
- Identify the main topic and retell key details of a text.
- Describe the connection between two individuals, events, ideas, or pieces of information in a text.
- Ask and answer questions about key details in a text.
- Retell stories, including key details, and demonstrate understanding of their central message or lesson.
- Describe characters, settings, and major events in a story, using key details.

Text Structure

- Ask and answer questions to help determine or clarify the meaning of words and phrases in a text.
- Know and use various text features (e.g., headings, tables of contents, glossaries, electronic menus, icons) to locate key facts or information in a text.
- Distinguish between information provided by pictures or other illustrations and information provided by the words in a text.
- Identify words and phrases in stories or poems that suggest feelings or appeal to the senses.
- Explain major differences between books that tell stories and books that give information, drawing on a wide reading of a range of text types.
- Identify who is telling the story at various points in a text.

Evaluate Text

- Use the illustrations and details in a text to describe its key ideas.
- Identify the reasons an author gives to support points in a text.
- Identify basic similarities in and differences between two texts on the same topic (e.g., in illustrations, descriptions, or procedures).
- Use illustrations and details in a story to describe its characters, setting, or events.
- Compare and contrast the adventures and experiences of characters in stories.

Writing Skills

Text Types and Purposes

- Write opinion pieces in which they introduce the topic or name the book they are writing about, state an opinion, supply a reason for the opinion, and provide some sense of closure.
- Write informative/explanatory texts in which they name a topic, supply some facts about the topic, and provide some sense of closure.
- Write narratives in which they recount two or more appropriately sequenced events, include some details regarding what happened, use temporal words to signal event order, and provide some sense of closure.

Produce and Publish Writing

- With guidance and support from adults, focus on a topic, respond to questions and suggestions from peers, and add details to strengthen writing as needed.
- With guidance and support from adults, use a variety of digital tools to produce and publish writing, including in collaboration with peers.

Research

- Participate in shared research and writing projects (e.g., explore a number of "how-to" books on a given topic and use them to write a sequence of instructions).
- With guidance and support from adults, recall information from experiences or gather information from provided sources to answer a question.

Language Skills

Conventions of Standard English

- Print all upper- and lowercase letters.
- Use common, proper, and possessive nouns.
- Use singular and plural nouns with matching verbs in basic sentences (e.g., He hops; We hop).
- Use personal, possessive, and indefinite pronouns (e.g., I, me, my, they, them, their, anyone, everything).
- Use verbs to convey a sense of past, present, and future (e.g., Yesterday I walked home; Today I walk home; Tomorrow I will walk home).

- Use frequently occurring adjectives.
- Use frequently occurring conjunctions (e.g., and, but, or, so, because).
- Use determiners (e.g., articles, demonstratives).
- Use frequently occurring prepositions (e.g., during, beyond, toward).
- Produce and expand complete simple and compound declarative, interrogative, imperative, and exclamatory sentences in response to prompts.
- Capitalize dates and names of people.
- Use end punctuation for sentences.
- Use commas in dates and to separate single words in a series.
- Use conventional spelling for words with common spelling patterns and for frequently occurring irregular words.
- Spell untaught words phonetically, drawing on phonemic awareness and spelling conventions.

Vocabulary

- Use sentence-level context as a clue to the meaning of a word or phrase.

- Use frequently occurring affixes as a clue to the meaning of a word.
- Identify frequently occurring root words (e.g., look) and their inflectional forms (e.g., looks, looked, looking).
- Sort words into categories (e.g., colors, clothing) to gain a sense of the concepts the categories represent.
- Define words by category and by one or more key attributes (e.g., a duck is a bird that swims; a tiger is a large cat with stripes).
- Identify real-life connections between words and their use (e.g., note places at home that are cozy).
- Distinguish shades of meaning among verbs differing in manner (e.g., look, peek, glance, stare, glare, scowl) and adjectives differing in intensity (e.g., large, gigantic) by defining or choosing them or by acting out the meanings.
- Use words and phrases acquired through conversations, reading and being read to, and responding to texts, including using frequently occurring conjunctions to signal simple relationships (e.g., because).

Contents

Contents

my alphabet

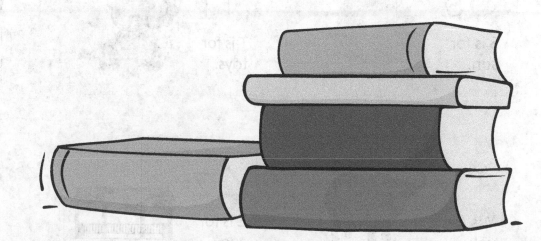

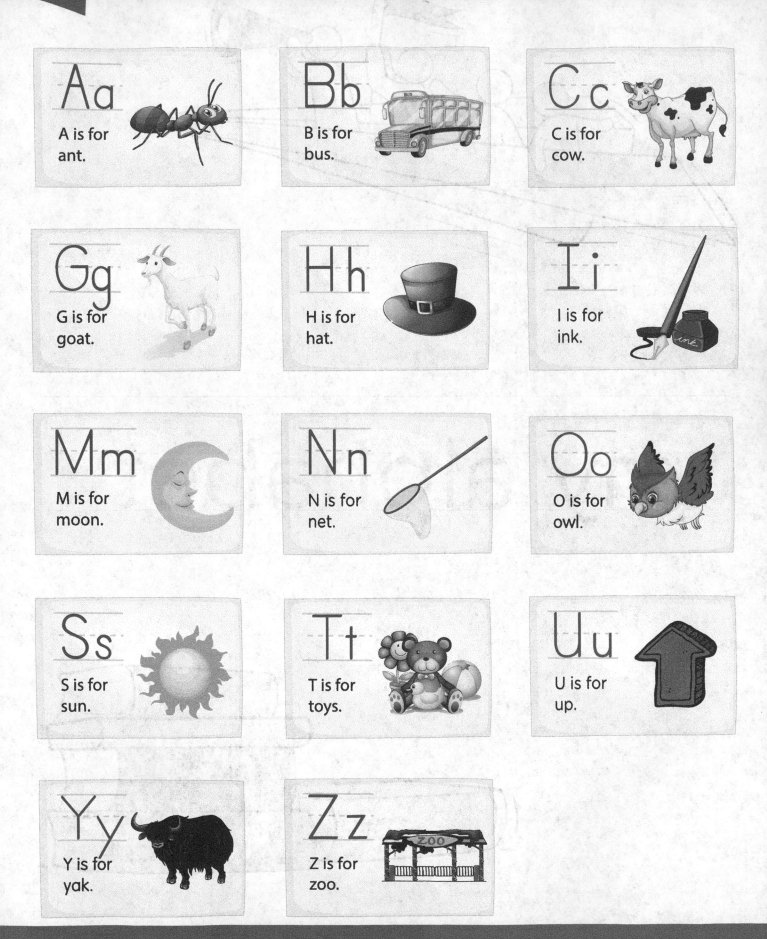

Aa
A is for ant.

Bb
B is for bus.

Cc
C is for cow.

Gg
G is for goat.

Hh
H is for hat.

Ii
I is for ink.

Mm
M is for moon.

Nn
N is for net.

Oo
O is for owl.

Ss
S is for sun.

Tt
T is for toys.

Uu
U is for up.

Yy
Y is for yak.

Zz
Z is for zoo.

X

Dd
D is for dog.

Ee
E is for eye.

Ff
F is for fox.

Jj
J is for jam.

Kk
K is for kite.

Ll
L is for lion.

Pp
P is for pig.

Qq
Q is for queen.

Rr
R is for rose.

Vv
V is for van.

Ww
W is for wave.

Xx
X is for xylophone.

Reading
Foundational
Skills

Phonics

Phonics is the ability to understand letters and their sounds. At the heart of phonics is the alphabet. While the letters always stay the same, letter sounds come in different combinations of vowels and consonants. You will work with your adult helper to review some of these combinations. Letter combinations affect the way a word is spoken.

Let's practice!

LEARNING SHORT AND LONG VOWEL SOUNDS

Have you ever blown into a whistle? If so, you can make short sounds by puffing air into the whistle. You can make long sounds by blowing hard into the whistle. Just like short and long sounds can be made from the same whistle, short and long vowel sounds can be made from the vowels.

Let's look at the examples below.

Short vowel sounds:

a as in c**a**t.	Miko's c**a**t is very friendly.
e as in l**e**t.	Paolo l**e**t Alison play first.
i as in h**i**t.	Alana h**i**t the ball.
o as in p**o**t.	The soup was cooked in a p**o**t.
u as in f**u**n.	Misha had f**u**n playing today.

Long vowel sounds:

a as in g**a**me.	Carlotta played a g**a**me with her sister.
e as in fr**ee**.	The bird was fr**ee** to fly away.
i as in d**i**me.	James found a d**i**me on the sidewalk.
o as in b**o**ne.	Darnell gave his dog a b**o**ne.
u as in t**u**ne.	Chen sang a t**u**ne about a mouse.

1. Circle the word with the **long vowel** sound.

   A. sit

   B. see

   C. sun

2. Circle the word with the **short vowel** sound.

   A. chip

   B. same

   C. fine

CONSONANT BLENDS

All the letters in the alphabet are consonants except for the vowels (a, e, i, o, u). Some words have consonants that team up together to make a sound. These teams are called consonant blends. They are made up of two or three letters. Each letter can be heard in a consonant blend.

Here are examples of these consonant blends:

bl as in **blue**

gl as in **glow**

dr as in **drop**

fr as in **from**

spr as in **spring**

Example: Say the word "frog."

Sound the word out one letter at a time. f r o g

The "**fr**" is a consonant blend. The "**f**" and the "**r**" make two separate sounds.

1. Fill in the blanks with a consonant team to make a word. Use the word bank at right to help you.

   A. _____ a c k

   B. ___ ___ a d

   C. _____ a g

word bank

bl

dr

gl

2. Circle the word with a consonant blend that has separate sounds for each letter.

   A. spray

   B. knock

   C. white

WORD PARTS

When you are learning to pronounce a new word, think of a train. It has an engine at the front, at least one car in the middle, and a caboose at the end. **One-syllable** words can be the same. They have one sound at the beginning, a vowel sound in the middle, and one more sound at the end.

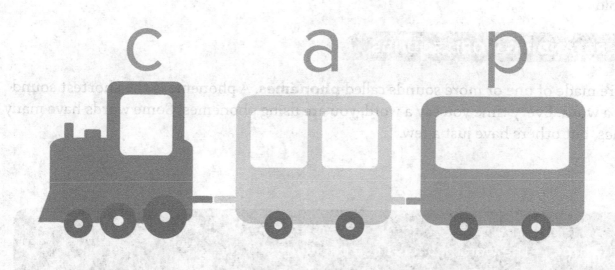

Example: Read the word cap slowly. Ask yourself these questions:

1. Does the **c** make a ***k*** sound?

2. Does the **a** make a short or long vowel sound?

3. Do you say the ***p*** sound?

Say the word slowly and then say it more quickly. Do you hear the different sounds when you speak it?

1. Circle the word with a vowel sound that sounds like the **a** in **ca̲p**?

    A. that

    B. dark

    C. gray

2. Which word has the same sound as the first letter in **cap**?

    A. chin

    B. cent

    C. cold

UNDERSTANDING WORD SOUNDS

Words are made of one or more sounds called **phonemes**. A phoneme is the shortest sound made in a word. Every time you say a word, you are using phonemes! Some words have many phonemes, but others have just a few.

Example: The word doll has three phonemes:

doll = d o l

The **d** makes one sound. The **o** makes the next sound.
The two **l's** together make only one sound.

The words below all have three phonemes. Write the phonemes into the blanks next to each word.

   A. kiss = __/__/__

   B. pack = __/__/__

   C. seem = __/__/__

Challenge: Circle the word with only two phonemes.

   A. know

   B. roll

   C. glue

Phonics and Word Recognition

The goal of mastering phonics is to help you to become good at figuring out the sounds in unfamiliar written words. When you see new words, it is important to use phonics skills to decode and understand them. The more you practice, the better your reading ability will become.

UNDERSTANDING DIGRAPHS

Digraphs are two consonants that make only one sound. They are found at the beginning of many words and also at the end of some words.

Digraphs can begin words:

ch – chain
CHān

sh – shark
SHärk

th – three
THrē

wh – wheel
(h)wēl

Digraphs can end words:

ch – switch
swiCH

sh – trash
traSH

th – earth
ərTH

ck – duck
dək

1. Fill in the blanks with the correct **digraph** from the word bank.

   A. Marco put his __ __ oes on his feet.

   B. A wagon has four __ __ eels.

   C. Zoe began to ri __ __ the bell.

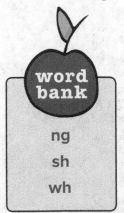

word bank

ng

sh

wh

Challenge:

The digraph **th** has two sounds:

th as in *thing*: The sound for this digraph comes only from your mouth.

th as in *them*: The sound for this digraph first comes from your throat as well as from your mouth.

Circle the words that use the digraph sound that comes only from your mouth.

   A. they

   B. third

   C. three

SPELLING REGULAR WORDS

Regular words are spelled the way they sound. Regular words often come from word families. Words from the same family have the same letters except for the beginning of each word.

Look at the different words that come from the **–at** word family.

b**at**	c**at**
ch**at**	f**at**
h**at**	p**at**
r**at**	th**at**

Activity 1

Write three words from the word family – *it*. Use the word bank below to help you out.

A. __ it

B. __ it

C. __ it

word bank

b	k
f	p
h	s

Activity 2

Some regular words have the same letters in them. Only the vowel is different.

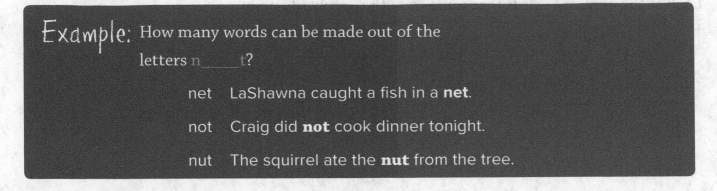

Example: How many words can be made out of the

letters n＿＿t?

net   LaShawna caught a fish in a **net**.

not   Craig did **not** cook dinner tonight.

nut   The squirrel ate the **nut** from the tree.

Make at least three words from the letters p＿t.
Use the word bank below to help you.

A. p＿t

B. p＿t

C. p＿t

word
bank

a
e
i
o
u

THE SILENT "–e"

How can you tell if a new word has a long vowel sound? For some words, there is a vowel in the middle and an **e** at the end. This **e** is called a silent **–e** because it is not heard by the reader. The silent **–e** tells you that the first vowel makes a long vowel sound.

Read the underlined words:

lake   Chiwetel swam in a <u>lake</u>.

kite   Marta flew a <u>kite</u>.

rope   Jermaine tied a <u>rope</u>.

huge   The mountain is <u>huge</u>.

1. Which letter is used at the end of each of the **underlined** words?_____

2. Is the letter at the end of the underlined words **silent**? _____

3. Is the vowel sound for each word **long** or **short**?_____

VOWEL TEAMS

There are five vowels in the alphabet:
a, e, i, o, u. Sometimes **y** can act as a vowel.
A **vowel team** is made up of two vowels. Some of these vowel teams can make long vowel sounds.

beads

ay makes long a.   **Stay** in your chair, please.

ea makes long e.   Maia wore a necklace of **beads**.

Match the word with the correct vowel sound.

1. pay   A. long o
2. lead   B. long e
3. coat   C. long a

Challenge: Make two words using the correct vowel teams from the word bank.

1. b___t

2. b___t

word bank

oo

oa

ue

A helpful hint to remember about vowel teams is that **when two vowels go walking, the first one does the talking**. So you would say the sound of the first vowel, while the other vowel stays silent.

VOWELS IN SYLLABLES

Every syllable must have a vowel sound that determines the number of syllables within the word.

Example: Look at how these words are broken into parts:

read = read (1 syllable)

maybe = may + be (2 syllables)

basketball = bas + ket + ball (3 syllables)

Activity 1

Circle the words that have more than one syllable. Rewrite each word and draw a line between each syllable.

   A. someone _____

   B. peanut _____

   C. goat _____

Activity 2

Match the word with the number of syllables it has.

   A. outside   1 syllable

   B. tomorrow   2 syllables

   C. paint   3 syllables

Digging Deeper

Write the names of five people you know. Draw a line between the syllables of each name. Have an adult help you if you are not sure where to draw the line. See who has the name with the most syllables. Then see if you have the name with the most syllables. How many syllables does your name have?

Sight Words

help	mother	someone	thing	night
baby	father	sometimes	please	know
their	aunt	something	little	would
look	uncle	important	laugh	come
were	with	grandmother	picture	done
said	what	grandfather	myself	two

UNDERSTANDING TWO-SYLLABLE WORDS

Learning how to read and understand words with **two syllables** may seem hard at first. Bigger words can be easier to understand if you break down each of their parts, or syllables, first. Some syllables use letters in a certain way that help you find the syllables in the word.

Here are a few:

> above = **a** + bove
>
> ever = **e** + ver
>
> oven = **o** + ven

Remember, every syllable has a vowel sound in it. A vowel sound can be made up of one or more vowels. A syllable does not have to have a consonant in it. Some two-syllable words begin with just a vowel sound that does not end with a consonant. The second syllable does begin with a consonant that is followed by a vowel sound.

Activity 1

Separate each word into its syllable parts. Then, circle the word that has a syllable with just one vowel in the syllable.

A. under

B. open

C. answer

Activity 2

Many words use the same letters next to each other. If these letters are together, that is often where the syllables are broken. Look at the words below and then read them out loud.

kitten = kit + ten

dinner = din + ner

village = vil + lage

Rewrite each word on the lines below. Draw a line between the double consonants. Then write the number of syllables next to the word.

A. funny _____

B. letter _____

C. yellow _____

CHANGING NOUNS BY THEIR ENDINGS

Most words have a *root*, or the main part of the word. You can change the word's meaning by adding different parts to its end. Word parts that are added to the end of a word are called **inflections**.

Example:

A noun is a person, place, or thing. In many sentences a noun does some kind of action in the sentence.

A dog can fetch a ball.

By adding **–s** to the word dog, you are now talking about more than one dog.

dog + s = dogs

Many dogs like to fetch balls.

Some nouns that end in **s** need to have **–es** to make them plural. These are nouns that end in **s**, **sh**, **(t)ch**, **zz**, *and* **x**.

bus + es = buses

All the school buses were parked in a row.

By adding **–es** to the word fox, you are now talking about more than one fox.

fox + es = foxes

Most foxes live in a forest.

Add –s or –es correctly to the nouns in the sentences below.

1. Max packed many box _____ before he moved to a new home.

2. Janelle named her two new cat _____ Boots and Twinks.

3. After school, Cameron greeted his mother with many kiss_____.

CHANGING VERBS BY THEIR ENDINGS

Verbs are words that show action. Action that is happening now is in the present tense. By adding **–s**, **–es,** or **–ing** to a verb, you can show action that is happening now. **–es** is added to verbs that end in **s**, **sh**, **(t)ch**, **zz**, and **x**.

Example: Alana **walks** to school every morning.

Julio **watches** the football game.

Zakaria is **playing** with her tablet.

Activity 1

Fill in the blank to make the words show action that is happening now.

1. Aoki play _____ in the park.

2. Joshua wash _____ the dishes.

3. The bee is buzz _____ in the garden.

Activity 2

What if you want to show action that has already happened?
You can do this by changing the end of the word to an **–ed**.

Example: Alana **walked** to school all last year.

Julio **watched** the football game yesterday.

Fill in the blank to make the words show action that has already happened.

1. Chen bake _____ a cake.

2. Misha jump _____ up and down.

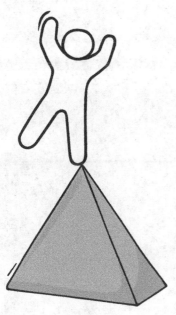

Reading Foundational Skills

Irregularly spelled words look different from the way they sound. They do not follow rules for spelling. You need to learn them by memorizing them. This can seem hard at first, but you can do it!

Many of the words you already know are irregularly spelled.

> Example 1: The word **one** sounds like **wun**.

Activity 1

Read the sentences below. Circle the correct spelling of the underlined words.

A. Wot/What book do you want to read next?

B. Sharon laft/laughed at the funny story.

C. Pablo heard a knock/nok on the door.

Activity 2

Match the words with how they sound.

1. busy   A. bild
2. build   B. bawt
3. bought   C. bizzy

Challenge: Circle the words that are spelled irregularly. *Hint:* These words are not spelled like they sound.

across   through   laugh

kite   once   know

night   open   paper

Fluency: Read with Purpose and Understanding

In this section, you will work with an adult as you practice and develop the art of fluent reading. Fluency means reading with speed, accuracy, and proper expression.

Take turns reading with your adult helper. As you read, remember to use the following strategies:

- Read the title and think of the story
- Look at the picture clues
- Start the word—say the beginning sounds
- Look for familiar parts in a word
- Reread to improve understanding and/or to improve fluency
- Read ahead and use the words after to help you figure out the unknown words

Adults:

Time your early achiever reading aloud for one minute, and cross out any words that were eliminated or misread. At the end of one minute, mark the last word read and allow your student to finish reading the text. Count the total number of errors and subtract that from the number of words read. This will give you the total number of words read per minute. Over an extended period of time, your student's fluency should increase by the number of words read per minute.

TOTAL NUMBER OF WORDS – NUMBER OF ERRORS = WORDS READ PER MINUTE

Unit 1 (September)	Unit 2 (December)	Unit 3 (March)	Unit 4 (June)
10	25	45	60

Thank You, Mrs. Spot!

Mrs. Spot likes to cook.	5
My friends and I want to look.	12
"What is in your big red pot?	19
May we have some, Mrs. Spot?"	25
Mrs. Spot likes to share.	30
"Come on kids, from over there!	36
Taste and see that it is good,	43
Take some home, if you would."	49
My friends and I like to eat.	56
At home we eat our treat so sweet.	64
"We must go back to Mrs. Spot,	71
To thank her for the food we got."	79
"Thank you, thank you Mrs. Spot!	85
We like to eat from your big red pot.	94
To show you that we thank you so,	102
We made you a gift with a big	110
Red bow!"	112

Words read in 1 minute – errors = WPM

CHECK FOR UNDERSTANDING

Adults: After your early achiever has finished reading, ask for a brief summary of the story so you can check comprehension. Write the summary on the lines below.

_____

_____

_____

GUIDED QUESTIONS

Use "Thank You, Mrs. Spot!" to answer the following questions.

1. What are two things that Mrs. Spot likes to do?

_____

_____

2. How do the kids feel about Mrs. Spot?

_____

_____

3. What kind of gift do you think the children gave to Mrs. Spot? Draw a picture in the space below.

A Bee Tale

I am a bumblebee black and yellow.	7
I am a very important fellow.	13
I give you many of the foods you eat,	22
Like honey, a treat so sweet.	28
When I give **pollen** to the crops and flowers,	37
They get most of their growing power.	44
Oranges, apples, pears, and limes—	49
Without me these would be gone in no time.	58
So the next time you see me flying by	67
Do not think I am just a pest in the sky.	78
For the important things I do each day,	86
Help you out in a special way!	93

Words read in 1 minute – errors = WPM

glossary

pollen: The very fine yellow dust that is made by a plant and carried to other plants of the same kind by wind or insects so that the plants can produce seeds.

CHECK FOR UNDERSTANDING

Adults: After your early achiever has finished reading, ask for a brief summary of the story so you can check comprehension. Write the summary on the lines below.

_____

_____

_____

GUIDED QUESTIONS

Use "A Bee Tale" to answer the following questions.

1. Why are bees important fellows?

   _____

2. What would be gone without bees?

   _____

3. Draw a picture of a bee bringing pollen to a flower.

Reading and Writing: Informational Texts

Maps and Globes

In this unit you will learn about maps and globes. You will understand how they connect to each other and that traveling becomes easy when you use them.

You will not be expected to know all of the words right now. Your adult helper can guide you. The more you practice, the easier it will be to recognize and understand new words.

Happy reading and writing!

How to Use Maps and Globes

1   What do you do if you are lost? How do you find your way to a place you have never been? You can use a map. A map is a tool that tells where places are located. There are many different types of maps. Maps can represent your block, neighborhood, or city. There are maps of states and countries as well.

2   On these maps you will find a tool called a **compass rose**. A compass rose is a guide that tells **direction**. Think of each direction as an arrow pointing. Directions are North, South, East, and West. A good way to remember this is to start at the top of the compass rose and say "**N**ever **E**at **S**oggy **W**affles" while going around like a clock. North points up. East points right. South points down. West points left.

3   A globe is another tool that tells where places are located. A **globe** is a ball-shaped **model** with a map of Earth on it. The green and brown parts show where the land is. The blue parts show the water. You can see all the countries and oceans on a globe. You may not be able to see all of these on a map. A globe can show us how the Earth spins.

4   A map is useful to help you get to where you need to go. It is flat and easy to fit into your bag. A globe will help you learn about the countries of the world. It is round like a ball. It is not as easy to take with you. Both maps and globes are important tools. They help you to find your way to many different places.

glossary

compass rose: A tool on a map used to show directions.

directions: North, South, East, West.

globe: A ball-shaped model of the earth.

model: A smaller version to show something that is large.

FINDING THE MAIN IDEA AND KEY DETAILS

Use "How to Use Maps and Globes" to answer the following questions.

1. Which sentence tells the **main idea** of this article?

   A. Maps could be a picture of your block, neighborhood, or city.

   B. Both maps and globes help you find many different places.

   C. A globe is a model of the Earth.

2. Which is a **key detail** that supports the main idea?

   A. A globe shows you how the Earth spins.

   B. A globe is round like a ball.

   C. A map is a picture of where you want to go.

3. How are a map and a globe the **same**?

   A. They both have streets on them.

   B. They are both tools that give directions.

   C. Both can fit easily in a bag or backpack.

4. How are a map and a globe **different**?

   _____

   _____

   _____

5. Label the directions on this compass rose.

Remember, the **main idea** is what the text is mostly about. **Key details** give support to the main idea.

CONNECTING IDEAS

Use "How to Use Maps and Globes" to answer the following questions.

1. What is a **compass rose**?
   A. A ball-shaped model of the Earth
   B. A smaller version to show something that is large
   C. A tool on a map used to show directions

2. Which word means "*a smaller version to show something that is large?*"
   A. model
   B. directions
   C. map

3. Which would you **not** find on a map?
   A. north
   B. compass rose
   C. globe

PICTURES HELP EXPLAIN A TEXT

Activity 1

1. You are at the **café**. What direction would you need to travel to get to the **zoo**?

    _____

2. You are at the school. In which **two** directions would you need to travel to get to the **park**?

    _____ and _____

Activity 2

Which would you use? A map or a globe?

1. You are at a campground and need to find the exit. _____

2. You want to know where oceans are. _____

3. You want something you can easily fit in your pocket. _____

4. You need to find a street in your city. _____

5. You want to see which country is the biggest. _____

6. You are trying to find the bears at the zoo. _____

COMPARE ILLUSTRATIONS AND TEXT

After reading "How to Use Maps and Globes," and looking at the picture below, complete the following activity. Read each sentence. If the information is found in the text, write **T**. If it is found in the picture, write **P**. If it is found in both write **B**.

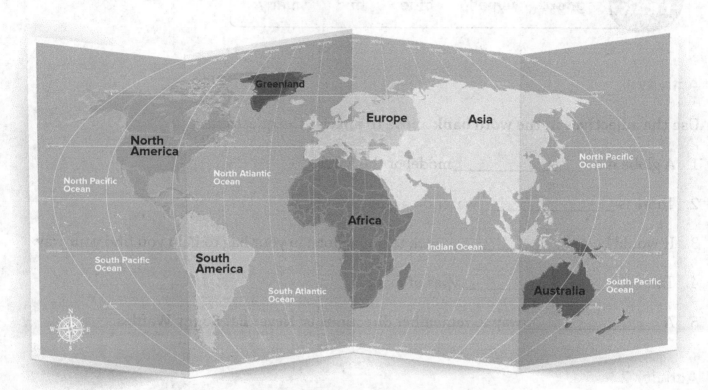

1. I learned the names of continents. _____

2. I learned what a compass rose is. _____

3. I learned that there are 7 oceans. _____

4. I learned that a globe shows how the Earth spins. _____

5. I learned that maps can show me a city neighborhood. _____

USING ADJECTIVES

An **adjective** is a word used to describe a person, place, thing, or idea. An adjective tells: *What kind? How many? Which one?*

word bank   good   small   blue   bad   many

Activity 1

Use the adjectives in the word bank above to answer the questions.

1. A globe is a _____ model of the Earth.

2. There is _____ water on a globe.

3. It would be a _____ idea to put a globe in your bag to help you find your way.

4. There are _____ types of maps.

5. A _____ way to remember directions is: **N**ever **E**at **S**oggy **W**affles.

Activity 2

Circle the adjective that fits best in the sentence.

1. I used the (round, flat) globe to find the North Pole.

2. Never eat (sweet, soggy) waffles.

3. Maps are (helpful, hard) tools.

USING COMMAS

> Example: **Commas (,)** are used in dates:
>
> **January 21, 2005**
>
> **Commas (,)** are used to separate words in a series:
>
> **milk, bread, and butter**

Activity 1

Place the missing commas in each sentence or date below.

1. December 31 2024

2. July 18 2021

3. I am going to the zoo park café and library.

Activity 2

Which answer uses commas correctly?

    A. We have a map globe, and a compass rose.

    B. June 21, 1948

    C. I have green, yellow and red, paint.

Activity 3

Which answer does not use commas correctly?

    A. My blanket is orange, brown, and green.

    B. May 20, 2014

    C. He baked, cookies bread and muffins.

Activity 4

Rewrite each item below, using commas properly.

1. August 8 2025_____

2. They like dolls cats and pink things. _____

USING ROOT WORDS

Words can be changed by adding **–ing, –ed, –s, –es,** or **–er** to the end. The **root**, or base word, is the part of the word from which other words can be made.

Example: talk + ing = **talking**

> **Talk** is the root word, ing is the ending.

want + ed = **wanted**

> **Want** is the root word, ed is the ending.

Adding –ing means that it is happening now

Adding –s or –es makes it plural

Adding –ed makes it past tense

Adding –er means you are comparing two things or a person is doing something

Circle the root word.

1. sleeping

2. buses

3. smaller

4. looked

5. walked

6. eats

7. talker

8. drawing

REAL-LIFE CONNECTIONS

Activity 1

Describe a time when you and your family used a map.

_____

_____

_____

_____

_____

_____

_____

_____

_____

Activity 2

Can you think of another way to remember the directions, North, South, East, and West? In the right order? The text uses **N**ever **E**at **S**oggy **W**affles. What else can you think of to help you remember this? Use words or phrases that mean something to you. Then it will be easier to remember.

_____

_____

Activity 3

A person who makes maps is called a *cartographer*. What kind of skills do you think a cartographer, or mapmaker needs? If you wanted to become a mapmaker, what subjects would you need to take in school?

_____

_____

WRITE YOUR NARRATIVE

Imagine you are a pirate. You are burying your treasure. You need to make a map showing where you buried it. Make up a story about how you got the treasure and how you plan to hide it. Use characters in your story, include details to describe actions, thoughts, and feelings. Be sure to include a beginning, middle, and ending in your story. When you're finished, draw your map!

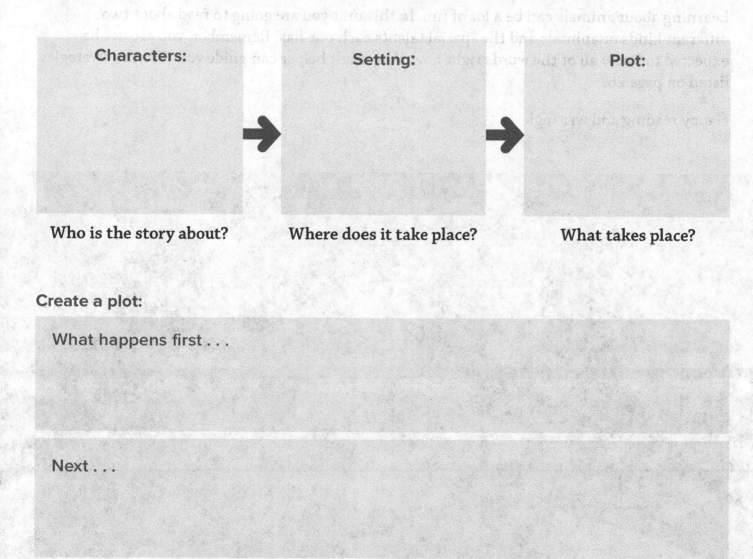

Characters:

Who is the story about?

Setting:

Where does it take place?

Plot:

What takes place?

Create a plot:

What happens first . . .

Next . . .

Finally, how does your story end?

Learning about animals can be a lot of fun. In this unit you are going to read about two different kinds of animals and the special talents each one has. Remember, you are not be expected to know all of the words right now. Your adult helper can guide you. Use the strategies listed on page 26.

Happy reading and writing!

Dolphin Diaries

Today, I met Mr. Wells. He knows about dolphins. I learned that people and dolphins do the same things in different ways.

Mr. Wells told us that dolphins work as a team to find food. Dolphins go fishing with the others in their <u>pod</u>. Half of the pod swims into a <u>school</u> of fish. The other half chases the fish closer to the rest of the pod. Dolphins can eat thirty pounds of fish a day!

I thought about last Saturday. I helped my mom in our garden. I picked a big bag of carrots. Mom held the bag for me. Together, we carried the bag to our kitchen. We worked as a team too!

Next, I learned how dolphins move in the water. Their fins and <u>flukes</u> help them to swim very fast. Dolphins hold their breath for up to thirty minutes! But they must come up to breathe air. Dolphins breathe with their blowholes.

I love to swim! I use my arms, legs, and feet when I swim. Sometimes, I hold my breath for twenty seconds underwater. Then I need to breathe air with my nose.

Finally, Mr. Wells said that dolphins <u>communicate</u>. They make clicking sounds. They can whistle. Dolphins also snuggle close to other dolphins in their pod.

Guess what? My dad showed me how to whistle yesterday! We had fun. I talk to my family every day! We talk about things I like to do. When I miss my parents, I give them a big hug. Sometimes I give them special cards.

glossary

communicate: To share information.

fluke: A dolphin's tail.

pod: A group of dolphins.

school: A group of fish.

FINDING THE MAIN IDEA AND DETAILS

After reading "Dolphin Diaries," complete the
graphic organizer.

Main Idea:

↓ ↓ ↓

Detail 1: | **Detail 2:** | **Detail 3:**

UNDERSTANDING VERBS

Verbs are divided into three main tenses: *past*, *present*, and *future*. Verb tense tells the reader *when* the action is taking place.

By simply adding an *–ed* to a word, the verb shows something that already happened.

The **present tense** tells readers the action is happening now.

Example: Ola is **playing** with the dolphin.

The **past tense** tells readers the action that has already happened.

Example: Ola **played** with the dolphin.

The future tense tells readers the action will happen in the future.

Example: Ola **will play** with the dolphin.

Activity 1

Rewrite each sentence so that the underlined verb is in the **past tense.**

1. I <u>use</u> my arms to swim.

   _____

2. I <u>learn</u> a new trick.

   _____

3. I <u>help</u> my mom in the garden.

   _____

4. I <u>show</u> my pod where to get food. _____

5. I <u>talk</u> to my dad. _____

Activity 2

Read each sentence. Write the word **past**, **present,** or **future** on the line next to the sentence to show the verb tense of the underlined verb.

1. I <u>learned</u> that people and dolphins do the same things in different ways.

   _____

2. Dolphins <u>show</u> their pod they love them by snuggling close.

   _____

3. The father <u>helped</u> his son learn to whistle! _____

4. I <u>will dig</u> in the garden. _____

USING END PUNCTUATION

There are three types of punctuation that end sentences: **period (.)**, **question mark (?)**, and **exclamation point (!)**.

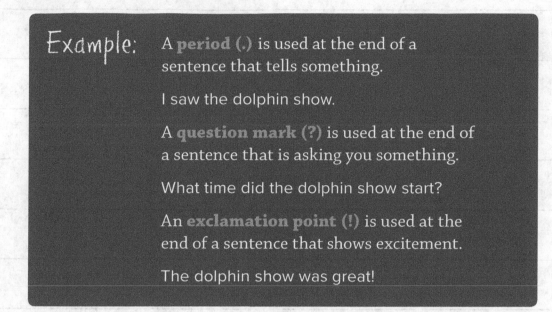

Example:

A **period (.)** is used at the end of a sentence that tells something.

I saw the dolphin show.

A **question mark (?)** is used at the end of a sentence that is asking you something.

What time did the dolphin show start?

An **exclamation point (!)** is used at the end of a sentence that shows excitement.

The dolphin show was great!

Circle the sentence that uses the correct end punctuation.

1. I went swimming yesterday?
   I went swimming yesterday.
   I went swimming yesterday!

2. Did you see the dolphin show?
   Did you see the dolphin show.
   Did you see the dolphin show!

3. Watch out, the dolphin is splashing water?
   Watch out, the dolphin is splashing water.
   Watch out, the dolphin is splashing water!

Challenge: Write *telling,* *asking,* and *excited* sentences.

_____

_____

_____

_____

_____

_____

_____

_____

_____

_____

_____

_____

_____

USING DIAGRAMS

Use the diagram of the dolphin to help answer the next set of questions.

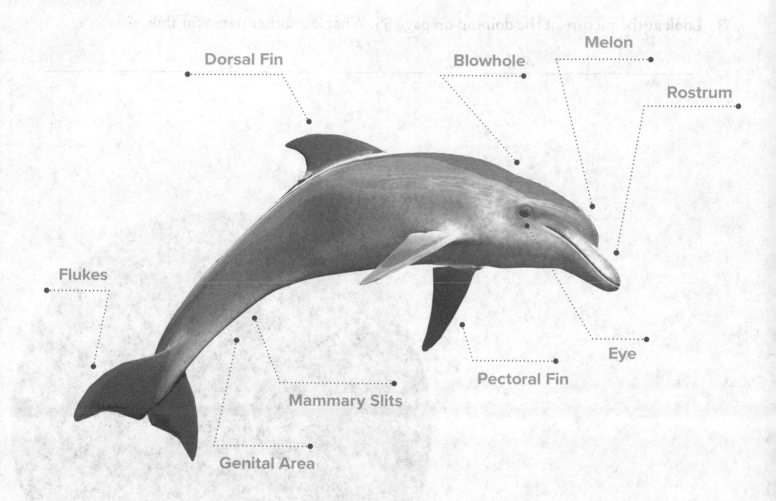

1. Look at the picture of the dolphin. On what part of the body is the blowhole located?

_____

2. Look at the picture of the dolphin on page 55. Which fins on a dolphin help it to swim the same way that arms help people to swim?

_____

3. Look at the picture of the dolphin on page 55. What is another name for flukes?

_____

An Elephant Essay

1 I am Esther, the elephant. I may look different from you. I may also be a lot bigger than you, but in some ways we are the same! Did you know that I use my <u>trunk</u> the same way that you use your voice, nose, arms, hands, fingers, or even a straw?

My Daily Habits

2 I live with my group, called a <u>herd</u>. We live in hot <u>climates</u>. We like to eat plants. In fact, I spend most of my day looking for and eating food. I use the end of my trunk just like you use fingers. I put food in my mouth with it. I'm always eating! I eat up to 300 pounds of food and drink 50 gallons of water every day! I use my trunk to help me drink. I suck the water up into it, and squirt it into my mouth. I also use my trunk to take a bath!

Things I Can Do

3 I am very strong. I use my trunk to tear down tree limbs. I also use it to pick up very tiny objects like marbles.

My Special Trunk

4 With my trunk, I <u>communicate</u>. I warn my friends of danger. I can punch if I need to <u>protect</u> myself. I can even communicate with a different herd several miles away with a special sound that humans cannot hear. When I greet my friends, we wrap our trunks together. Using my trunk, I smell other elephants. Then I know how my friend feels. I like to stick close to my herd. Being an elephant is fun!

glossary

climate: Weather conditions.

communicate: To share information.

herd: A group of elephants who live together.

protect: To keep safe from harm.

trunk: An elephant's long nose.

UNDERSTANDING TEXT FEATURES

Use "An Elephant Essay" to answer the following questions.

1. What is the title of the article?

   _____

2. Under which subheading can you find information on how an elephant communicates?
   A. Things I Can Do
   B. My Daily Habits
   C. My Special Trunk

3. Using the glossary, which word means a *group of elephants*?
   A. protect
   B. communicate
   C. herd

Text features are details an author uses to give more information. These can be titles, pictures, subheadings, glossaries, or captions.

COMPARING DIFFERENT TYPES OF INFORMATION

Using "An Elephant Essay," and the pictures below, answer the following questions.

1. What do you learn about elephants when you look at the pictures below?

   _____

   _____

   _____

2. Where can you find specific information about where elephants live?

   A. The text
   B. The pictures
   C. Both

3. Where can you find information about what elephants eat?

   A. The text

   B. The pictures

   C. Both

COMPARING AND CONTRASTING ARTICLES

After reading, "Dolphin Diaries" and "An Elephant Essay," describe how the articles are alike and different. Use the Venn diagram below.

Dolphin Diaries (different)

Similar

An Elephant Essay (different)

COMPARING CHARACTERISTICS

In the chart below, place the following words or phrases from the word bank in the correct columns.

word bank

trunk

rostrum

eats a lot

stays with their group

shows love

drinks 50 gallons of water a day

eats plants

communicates

holds breath for 30 minutes

fluke

can pick up marbles

swims

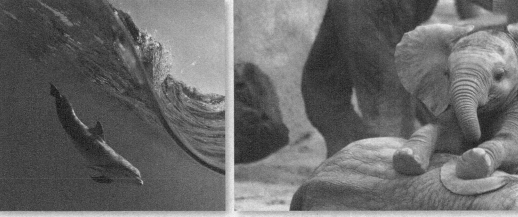

Dolphins	Elephants	Both

WRITE YOUR OPINION

Dolphins and elephants both lead interesting lives. If you could be one of these animals for a day, which one would you choose and why?

Write an opinion essay stating your answers. Be sure your essay has a topic sentence (or main idea) that tells your opinion. Next, list three reasons why you want to be that animal. Finally, write a conclusion that restates your opinion. Use the graphic organizer below to plan your essay.

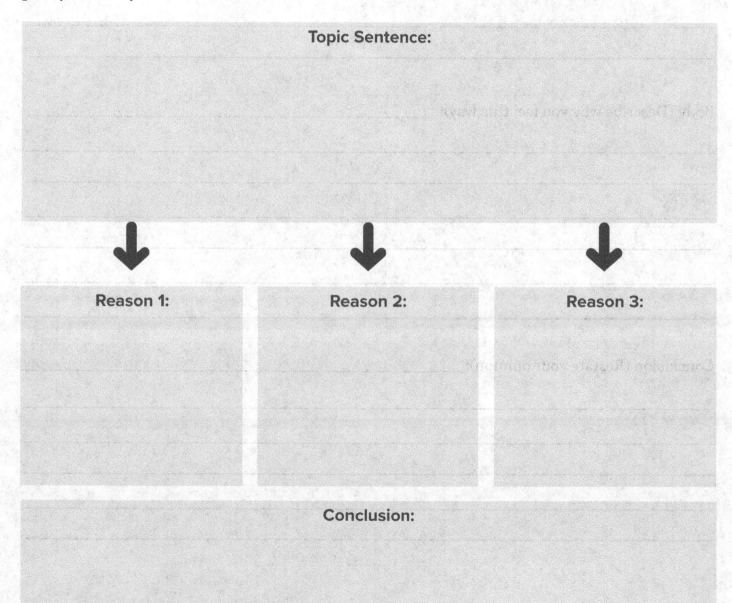

Topic Sentence:

Reason 1:

Reason 2:

Reason 3:

Conclusion:

Use your outline from page 63 to develop your work below. Plan an introduction, a body with your facts, and a conclusion.

Introduction (Opinion sentence): _____

_____

_____

_____

_____

Body (Describe why you feel this way): _____

_____

_____

_____

_____

_____

_____

Conclusion (Restate your opinion): _____

_____

_____

_____

_____

_____

Remember to use your *My Journal* pages at the back of the workbook if you need more space to write.

REVIEW

Congratulations! You have completed the lessons in this section. Now you will have the opportunity to practice some of the skills you just learned.

Reading Fluency

Adults: Time early achiever reading aloud for one minute. Make a note of where your student is at the end of one minute. (Your student should be able to read 10–60 words per minute.) Then, have your student continue reading to the end of the text to answer the questions that follow.

Tablet Dolphin

Dolphins are very smart. They talk to each other by making sounds with	13
their blowholes. We can hear some of these sounds. But there are other	26
sounds that we cannot hear. Each dolphin has a different sound, in the	39
same way that you and I have different names. A baby dolphin can pick	53
out its mother's special sound.	58
We can use computers to learn how dolphins talk. A tablet was used to	72
test a baby dolphin named Merlin [mur–lin]. Merlin was shown an object.	84
With his beak, he touched the same picture of the object on the tablet's	98
screen. A **microphone** recorded the sounds he made. People will study	109
these sounds.	111
Some people are working on an **app** to create dolphin sounds. Then,	123
people and dolphins could talk to each other! A tablet is a good tool. With	138
it, we will learn more about our animal friends.	147

Words read in 1 minute – errors = WPM

Activity 1

Circle the correct verb in each sentence.

1. Merlin (use/used) his beak to choose the picture.

2. A microphone records the sounds that he (makes/making).

3. Dolphins (will talk/talking) to each other using special sounds that people cannot hear.

Activity 2

Fill in the blank with an adjective of your choice to complete the sentence.

1. Dolphins like to swim in the _____ water.

2. Baby dolphins are _____ .

3. _____ boats sometimes bump into dolphin pods.

Activity 3

Use the correct end punctuation in the following sentences.

1. The scientist wants to talk to dolphins

2. Did you hear the dolphin noises

3. Dolphins are amazing

glossary

app: Application downloaded to mobile devices used for a specific purpose.

microphone: A device used to help record sounds.

tablet: A handheld touchscreen computer.

Activity 4

Circle the root word in each bolded word. Write the past tense of the bolded word on the next line.

1. My friend is **watching** the dolphin show.

   Past tense: My friend _____ the dolphin show.

2. Jamie was **looking** at the elephants on the nature show.

   Past tense: Jamie _____ at the elephants on the nature show.

3. We are **helping** the animal find a home.

   Past tense: We _____ the animal find a home.

Activity 5

For each word, place a checkmark beside the person's or animal's quality.

	Mammal	Breathe air	Fins	Hair	Live on land	Eat fish	Eat plants
Elephant							
Dolphin							
Human							

An Artist Named Ruby

Do you like to paint? Painting can be fun. Did you know that some animals also like to paint? Listen to the story about a special elephant, named Ruby.

In 1974, Ruby was taken from her home in Thailand (sounds like TIE-LAND) and sent to live in the Phoenix (sounds like FEE-NIX) Zoo. She was the only elephant in the zoo. Since elephants like to stay with their **herd**, Ruby was very lonely and unhappy for many years. To pass the time, Ruby made stick drawings. She grabbed sticks and made lines in the dirt. A zookeeper named Tawny noticed this. Tawny decided to give Ruby some paint and paintbrushes.

With a little help from the zookeeper, Ruby could paint! The zookeeper would show her different colors of paint. Ruby would choose a color. The zookeeper would help dip the paintbrush into the paint. Ruby held the paintbrush in her trunk. She painted on a **canvas**. It took about 10 minutes for her to finish a painting. Then Ruby put her name on it. The zookeeper would give her a black marker. Ruby would make a black line.

Ruby's paintings became **famous**. They sold for a lot of money. The money was used to help animals and zoos. Ruby helped a lot of animals!

glossary

canvas: A white board that artists paint on.

famous: Well-known.

herd: A group of elephants.

Activity 1

After reading "An Artist Named Ruby," answer the questions below.

1. What is the title of this article?_____

    _____

    _____

2. What is a canvas? Why is it important in Ruby's story? _____

    _____

    _____

3. What information does the picture on page 70 show that is not in the article? _____

    _____

    _____

    _____

4. Ruby and Merlin are both special animals. After reading "An Artist Named Ruby" and "Tablet Dolphin," describe why both of these animals are important.

    _____

    _____

    _____

Activity 2

After reading "An Elephant Essay" and "An Artist Named Ruby," describe how the articles are similar and different. Complete the Venn diagram below.

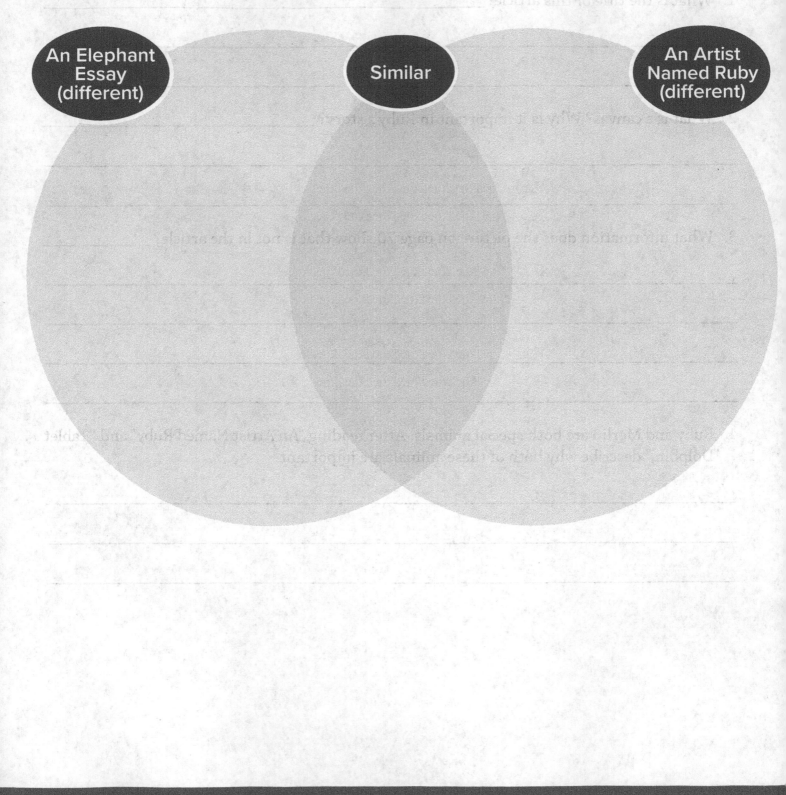

An Elephant Essay (different)

Similar

An Artist Named Ruby (different)

DISCOVER

Write Your Story

Choose an animal that you like. Pretend that animal has a special talent. What would it be? Write about a day in the life of that animal. Use characters in your story and include details to describe actions, thoughts, and feelings. Be sure to include a beginning, middle, and ending in your story.

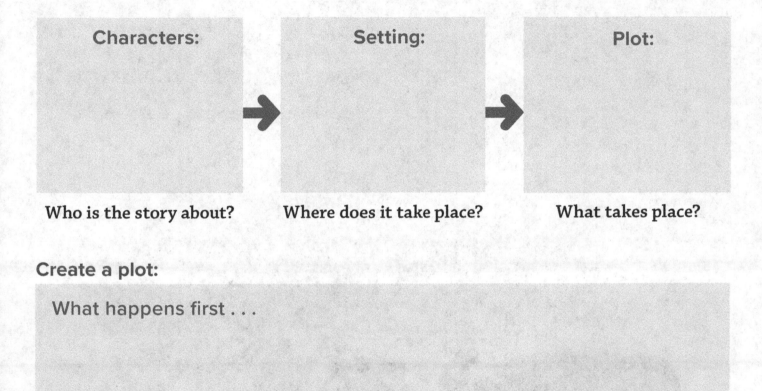

Characters: → **Setting:** → **Plot:**

Who is the story about?   Where does it take place?   What takes place?

Create a plot:

What happens first . . .

Next . . .

Then . . .

Finally, how does your story end?

Write Your Story

Use your outline from pages 73–74 to develop your work below. Plan an introduction, a body with your plot, and a conclusion.

Introduction (Set up your story. Who is in it? Where and when is it set?):

_____

_____

_____

_____

_____

Body (Describe what happens in your story): _____

_____

_____

_____

_____

_____

Conclusion (How does your story end?): _____

_____

_____

_____

_____

_____

Reading plus active teaches us about the history and people before us. Best of all, the stories in this section are not only valuable life lessons, but also show us information which further highlights the stories with your adult helpers.

Reading and Writing: Literature

Folktales

Reading literature teaches us about the different ways that people behave. Even though the stories in this section are not real, valuable life lessons can be learned. Pay attention as you read through the stories with your adult helper.

WHAT IS A FOLKTALE?

In this unit, you will read two versions of The Three Bears, a folktale from the country of England. A folktale is a story that is passed from person to person over hundreds of years. Each person may tell the story a little differently, making it more interesting. Folktales represent the culture and customs of the people from which they came. As you read with your adult helper, remember to use your reading strategies. Read the title and think of the story.

- Look at the picture clues.
- Start the word—say the beginning sounds.
- Look for familiar parts in a word.
- Reread to improve understanding and/or to improve fluency.
- Read ahead and use the words after to help you figure out the unknown words.

The Story of the Three Bears

Long ago, a big bear, a medium-sized bear, and a small bear lived together in a house. One morning, they made **porridge** for breakfast. The porridge was too hot to eat right away. They put it in bowls on the table. Then they went on a walk and waited for it to cool down.

While the bears were out walking, a girl named Goldilocks came to their house. She was a very **curious** little girl. She also did not have good **manners**. She walked right into the house! She saw the porridge on the table. There was a big bowl, a medium-sized bowl, and a small bowl. Goldilocks was hungry, so she tried all three bowls. The porridge in the big bowl was too hot. The porridge in the medium-sized bowl was too cold. The porridge in the small bowl was just right. She ate it all up!

After she ate, Goldilocks wanted to sit down. She saw a big chair, a medium-sized chair, and a small chair. The big chair was too hard. The medium-sized chair was too soft. The small chair was just right. But while she was sitting, the chair fell apart!

Then she wanted to take a nap. In the bedroom she saw a big bed, a medium-sized bed, and a small bed. The big bed was too high on one end. The medium-sized bed was too high on the other end. The small bed was just right, and Goldilocks fell asleep.

When the bears returned, they could tell that someone was in their house. "Someone ate some of my porridge!" said the big bear. "Someone ate some of my porridge, too!" said the medium-sized bear. "Someone ate ALL of my porridge!" said the small bear.

Then the bears saw their chairs. "Someone sat in my chair!" said the big bear. "Someone sat in my chair, too!" said the medium-sized bear. "Someone sat in my chair, and they BROKE it!" said the small bear.

Finally, the bears went into the bedroom. "Someone was in my bed!" said the big bear. "Someone was in my bed, too!" said the medium-sized bear. "Look! Someone is STILL in my bed!" said the small bear. Just then, Goldilocks woke up. All three of the bears were looking at her. She was so scared that she leaped up from the small bear's bed. She jumped out the window and ran away as fast as she could. The three bears never saw her again.

glossary

curious: Wanting to know or learn new things.

manners: Polite behavior; a way of doing things that is right and respectful to others.

porridge: A mushy food made of grains boiled in water or milk, such as oatmeal.

CHARACTERS, SETTINGS, AND EVENTS

Use "The Story of the Three Bears" to answer the following questions.

1. Where is the setting of the story?
   A. Goldilocks' house
   B. The bears' house
   C. Outside of a house

2. What is one **problem** the bears have in the story?_____
   _____

3. Goldilocks walks into the bears' house without asking. What does that tell you about her?
   _____

   _____

4. Put these events from the story in the right order by numbering them from 1 to 4.

 _____

 _____

 _____

_____

WHO IS TELLING THE STORY?

Use "The Story of the Three Bears" to answer the following questions.

> Sometimes a story is **narrated**, or told, by one of the characters in the story. Other times, a story is told by someone else who is not in the story, like the author.

1. Who is **narrating** "The Story of the Three Bears?"

   A. Goldilocks   B. One of the Bears   C. The author

2. When characters in a story talk, the things they say are called **dialogue**. Why do you think the author used different sizes of words for the dialogue in this story?

_____

SPELLING

Use your knowledge of common spelling patterns to fill in the missing word in each sentence, using the picture as a clue.

1. Goldilocks had curly yellow _____.
   Hint: When two vowels go walking, the first one does the talking.

2. She walked right through the bears' front _____.
   Hint: This vowel team makes one long sound.

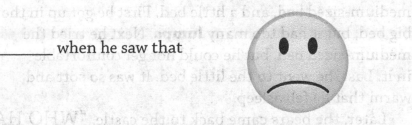
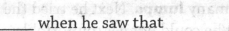

3. She ate porridge with a _____.
   Hint: This vowel team makes one long sound.

4. The small bear was _____ when he saw that his porridge was gone.
   Hint: This word has one syllable.

Scrapefoot

Once upon a time, three bears lived in a castle in the woods. One was a great big bear, one was a medium-sized bear, and one was a little bear. A fox also lived in the woods, and his name was Scrapefoot. He was **afraid** of the bears, but he wanted to know more about them. So, one day Scrapefoot went to the castle. He opened the door a little bit and stuck his head inside. No one was home! He went all the way inside the castle.

The first thing he saw was three chairs. There was a big chair, a medium-sized chair, and a little chair. He sat down in the big chair. It was very hard and uncomfortable! Next he tried the medium-sized chair. It was uncomfortable, too. At last he sat down in the little chair. It was soft, warm, and very comfortable. But all of a sudden, the little chair broke!

Scrapefoot got up and looked around some more. He saw a table with three bowls of milk. There was a big bowl, a medium-sized bowl, and a little bowl. He was thirsty, so he took a sip of the milk in the big bowl. It was so sour that he could not drink any more! Next he tasted the milk in the medium-sized bowl. That milk was not good, either. Finally he tried the milk in the little bowl. It was good and sweet. Scrapefoot drank it until it was gone.

Then Scrapefoot went upstairs. He found a big bed, a medium-sized bed, and a little bed. First he got up in the big bed, but it had too many **lumps**. Next he tried the medium-sized bed, but he could not get comfortable in it. Last, he went to the little bed. It was so soft and warm that he fell asleep.

Later, the bears came back to the castle. "WHO HAS BEEN SITTING IN MY CHAIR?" said the big bear. "WHO HAS BEEN SITTING IN MY CHAIR?" said the medium-sized bear. "Who has been sitting in my chair, and has broken

it?" said the little bear. Then the bears went to drink their milk. "WHO HAS BEEN DRINKING MY MILK?" said the big bear. "WHO HAS BEEN DRINKING MY MILK?" said the medium-sized bear. "Who has been drinking my milk, and has drunk it all up?" said the little bear. Finally, the bears went upstairs to the bedroom. "WHO HAS BEEN SLEEPING IN MY BED?" said the big bear. "WHO HAS BEEN SLEEPING IN MY BED?" said the medium-sized bear. "Who has been sleeping in my bed—look, there he is!" said the little bear.

The bears picked Scrapefoot up by his feet. They swung him back and forth, back and forth, and threw him out the window. Now Scrapefoot was awake! He was so scared that he ran away as fast as he could. He never went near the castle again.

glossary

afraid: Feeling fear, scared.

lump: A bump or bulge.

WHO IS TELLING THE STORY?

Use "Scrapefoot" to answer the following questions.

1. Who is the narrator, or one telling the story, in "Scrapefoot?"
   A. The author
   B. Scrapefoot
   C. The big bear

2. How can you tell the difference between what the characters say and what the narrator is telling you?

   _____

3. Which character does not say anything in the story?
   A. Scrapefoot
   B. The big bear
   C. The medium-sized bear

4. In the space below, write one thing that the little bear says.

   _____

COMPARING AND CONTRASTING STORIES

1. Which character from "The Story of the Three Bears" is the character of Scrapefoot the fox most like?
   A. The little bear
   B. The big bear
   C. Goldilocks

When you compare two or more things, you are trying to find out how they are alike, or similar. When you contrast two or more things, you are trying to find out how they are different.

Now that you have read "The Story of the Three Bears" and "Scrapefoot," describe how the two stories are the same and different. Fill in the chart below:

"The Story of the Three Bears" (different)	Both (similar)	"Scrapefoot" (different)

USING DETERMINERS

word bank

a

the

this

that

these

those

The words in this word bank are called **determiners**. A determiner answers the question, *which one*?

The is used when you are talking about something specific, like the story of "Scrapefoot." **A** is used when you are talking about something that is not specific. So, **a** story could be **any** story, not just "Scrapefoot."

This, **that**, **these**, and **those** are **determiners** that tell **how many** things you are talking about and **how close** or **far away** they are. The chart below shows when each word should be used:

Determiner	How many things?	Where?
This	One thing	Close, nearby
These	More than one thing	Close, nearby
That	One thing	Not close, far away
Those	More than one thing	Not close, far away

Circle the right determiner for each sentence in this short paragraph based on the story:

   One day, Scrapefoot went into **(the/that)** bears' castle. He saw three bowls of milk on **(those/a)** table. He drank some milk from the smallest bowl. "**(These/This)** milk is good!" he said. He went into the bedroom to take **(a/that)** nap. "**(These/This)** beds look comfortable!" he said. Scrapefoot fell asleep in **(a/the)** smallest bed. The three bears came home. **(This/Those)** bears were not happy to find Scrapefoot in their castle. "Look at **(that/a)** fox over there in my bed!" the small bear said. The bears picked up Scrapefoot and threw him out of the castle.

UNDERSTANDING THE CLUES

You might not know all of the words that are in a story. But by looking at other words in the sentence around them, you can find clues, or hints, to what they mean.

In these four sentences from the story, the bolded word is a word that you may not know. The underlined words in each sentence, though, can give you clues to what the bolded word means. Using the clues, tell what each word means.

1. "It was soft, warm, and very **comfortable**."

   _____

2. "He was **thirsty**, so he took a sip of the milk in the big bowl."

   _____

3. "It was so **sour** that he could not drink any more!"

   _____

4. "He was so **scared** that he ran away as fast as he could."

   _____

Reading and Writing: Literature

WRITE YOUR EXPLANATION

An explanation is written to explain how or why something happens. A good explanation should have an introduction, or beginning, that grabs the reader's attention. There should also be plenty of facts and details that support the main idea, or topic, of the explanation. A conclusion, or ending, is used to complete the explanation of the topic.

After reading "Scrapefoot," use the organizer to plan a short, one-paragraph essay that explains the story and tells why the three bears throw Scrapefoot out the window at the end of the story.

Title of your paragraph:

Introduction (sentence that tells the main idea you will be writing about):

Supporting fact #1 (detail from the story):

Supporting fact #2 (detail from the story):

Supporting fact #3 (detail from the story):

Conclusion (sentence that restates the main idea you wrote about):

Fables are the most well-known stories with morals. Fables are usually short stories featuring animals with human thoughts and qualities. A moral is a life lesson that the story teaches. Remember to write down the lessons you learn and share them with your friends.

Happy reading!

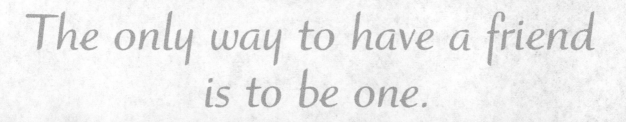

The only way to have a friend
is to be one.

The Happy Prince

Once upon a time, a very tall **statue** of a prince looked over a city. The statue had two blue **sapphire** eyes. Everyone in the city called the statue the Happy Prince.

One day, a swallow flew into the city. He was flying south for the winter. It was a long trip. The swallow needed a place to sleep. He landed on the foot of the Happy Prince. "I will stay here tonight," he said.

Suddenly, a drop of water landed on the swallow's head. He looked up at the statue. It was crying! "Why are you crying?" the swallow asked.

"People call me the Happy Prince, but I am not happy at all," the statue said. "I am so tall that I can see the whole city. I see people who need help, but no one helps them. I want to help, but I am a statue. I cannot move. That is why I am crying. Swallow, will you help me?"

"I will help you tonight, but tomorrow I must fly south. What should I do?" the swallow asked.

"Please take one of my sapphires," the prince answered. "Fly to the sick boy over there. Give it to his mother. Then she will have money to take him to the doctor."

The swallow was **shocked**. "That sapphire is your eye! I cannot take your eye!"

But the prince said, "Please take it. I will still have one left. The boy is more important." So the swallow took the sapphire and gave it to the boy's mother. She was so happy!

The next day the prince said, "Swallow, will you help me again?"

The swallow wanted to fly away. Instead he said, "Yes, I will help you one more time. What should I do?"

"See that girl? She has no warm clothes for winter. Please, take the other sapphire to her. Then she will have money to buy warm clothes."

The swallow was very sad. "Prince, if I do that, you will not be able to see."

"I know," the prince said, "but the girl is more important. Please do this for me, Swallow!" So the swallow took the sapphire to the girl. She was very happy. Then he flew back to the statue.

"I know you must go now," the prince said. "Thank you for helping me."

But the swallow said, "Prince, you gave up your eyes to help other people. I cannot leave you now. I will stay here, and tell you what I see. I will be your eyes." The swallow kept his promise. He stayed with the prince for the rest of his life.

glossary

sapphire: A blue gemstone that can be worth a lot of money.

shocked: Strongly surprised or upset.

statue: A piece of art made of stone or metal, often in the shape of a human.

FINDING THE CENTRAL MESSAGE AND KEY DETAILS

Use "The Happy Prince" to answer the following questions.

1. Who are the main **characters** in the story?

   _____

   _____

2. At the beginning of the story, what is the swallow's goal, or the main thing he is trying to do?

   A. Find sad people that he can help

   B. Fly south for the winter

   C. Become the prince's friend

3. What is the swallow's new goal at the end of the story?

   _____

   _____

4. Why does the Happy Prince say he is not really happy?

   A. Because the swallow does not want to help him

   B. Because people took both of his sapphire eyes

   C. Because he sees sad things going on in the city

5. These events from the story are in the wrong order. Put them in the right order by writing the correct number (1, 2, or 3) in the space.

   A. The swallow gives a sapphire to a little girl   _____

   B. The swallow promises to stay with the prince   _____

   C. The swallow gives a sapphire to a sick boy's mother   _____

6. Which character learns a lesson in the story?

    A. The swallow

    B. The Happy Prince

    C. The sick boy's mother

7. What **lesson** does that character learn?

    A. If you give things to people, they will always want more from you.

    B. Giving to others is better than always thinking about yourself.

    C. Money is always the best thing you can give to someone.

WORDS THAT TELL ABOUT FEELINGS

1. What does the bolded word in this sentence from the story tell you about how the prince feels?

    *"He looked up at the statue. It was **crying**!"*

    _____

2. What word does the story use to tell how the little girl feels when she gets the sapphire?

    A. Surprised   B. Happy   C. Thankful

3. Look at the definitions, or meanings, of the three words in the glossary. Which of the three words would you use to tell how someone feels?

    A. Statue   B. Sapphire   C. Shocked

4. Underline the **feeling** word(s) in the following sentence from the story:

    "The swallow was very sad."

PICTURES HELP WITH UNDERSTANDING

Use "The Happy Prince" to answer the following questions.

1. Look at the picture on page 92, from the story. Which event happened *before* the event in the illustration?

    A. The swallow felt the Happy Prince's teardrop fall on his head.

    B. The swallow gave the Happy Prince's eye to a little girl.

    C. The swallow promised to stay with the Happy Prince.

2. What objects, or things, from the story are shown in this picture to the right?

    _____

    How do you know?

    _____

    _____

3. The word **swallow** has several definitions, or meanings. Based on what you see in the illustrations on pages 92 and 93, which definition of **swallow** is being used in the story?

    A. To cause food to go from the mouth to the stomach

    B. A small bird with long, pointed wings and a forked tail

    C. The amount that can be consumed or gulped at one time

USING PREPOSITIONS

Here are some prepositions that you have probably seen and used before:

word bank

to

on

around

from

with

Use the prepositions from the word bank to fill in the blanks in these sentences about "The Happy Prince."

1. The swallow landed _____ the statue of the Happy Prince.

2. He took the sapphire _____ the prince and gave it _____ the little girl.

3. The swallow stayed _____ the prince.

4. The prince could see all _____ the city.

PUNCTUATING SENTENCES

Use a period, question mark, or exclamation mark to add the correct end punctuation to the sentences below.

1. Why are you crying _____

2. The bird stayed with the prince _____

3. Will you help me _____

4. I cannot take your eye away _____

5. Thank you so much for this sapphire _____

6. The statue was called the Happy Prince _____

PREFIXES

Many new words can be made by adding special beginnings and endings to words that already exist.

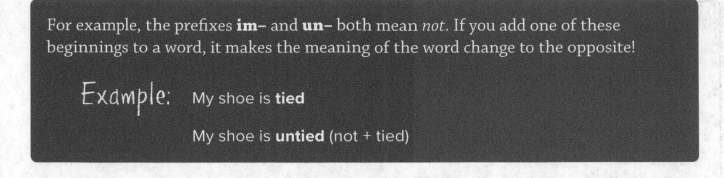

For example, the prefixes **im–** and **un–** both mean *not*. If you add one of these beginnings to a word, it makes the meaning of the word change to the opposite!

Example: My shoe is **tied**

My shoe is **untied** (not + tied)

Using what you know about common English words, use one of the beginnings im– or un– along with the word provided to complete each sentence below.

1. The Happy Prince was _____ (not happy).

2. "It is _____ (not possible) for me to take your eye, Prince!" said the swallow.

3. The prince thought it was _____ (not fair) that no one was helping the sad people in his city.

4. The prince was _____ (not able) to help people by himself because he could not move.

USING CONJUNCTIONS

Some words are used to show relationships between events or ideas.

> **Example:** "The swallow stopped in the city **because** he needed a place to spend the night."

The sentence has two ideas: 1) The swallow stopped in the city, and 2) He needed a place to spend the night.

The word **because** connects those ideas.

Common conjunctions can be remembered as **F-A-N-B-O-Y-S**:

for and nor but or yet so

In each of the following sentences, underline the conjunction.

1. The swallow said he would help the prince, but only for one night.

2. The little boy's mother was happy after the swallow gave her the sapphire.

3. The prince was crying, so the swallow agreed to help him.

4. The swallow wanted to fly south for the winter, yet he stayed with the prince.

Challenge: Write a sentence on a topic of your choice, using at least one conjunction.

_____

_____

WRITE YOUR OPINION

Did you like the story, "The Happy Prince?" Use the organizer to plan out how you will write your opinion.

My opinion is:

The reason(s) I think (your opinion) is/are because (list reasons):

Supporting detail:

Supporting detail:

Supporting detail:

Conclusion (sentence that restates the main idea you wrote about):

Now that you have a plan for your writing, imagine that you have been asked to write a review of the story, "The Happy Prince," for a magazine. Use the information from your graphic organizer to give your opinion about the story and state reasons. Remember to include linking words in your letter to connect your ideas. Try using the following linking words: *because, and, also.*

Introduction (Opinion sentence):

_____

_____

_____

_____

_____

Body (Describe why you feel this way):

_____

_____

_____

_____

_____

_____

Conclusion (Restate your opinion):

_____

_____

_____

_____

_____

Poetry

In this unit, you will read a nonfiction poem. Nonfiction writing is true. It is about real people, places, or events. You will imagine you are walking in the woods, seeing and hearing different things.

Put your imagination caps on, and let's get started!

A Walk in the Woods

Walking in the woods
There's a lot to see and do.
You could spot a busy squirrel
And maybe chase it, too.

You might hear a woodpecker
Tapping on the trees,
Or taste the sweet, sweet honey
Of a **swarm** of yellow bees.

Walking in the woods,
You might stop and smell a flower,
Or step beneath a passing cloud
And get a **chilly** shower.

You could dig up slimy worms
And hold them in your hand.
Just please don't visit Mr. Skunk
With his **perfume** so grand!

glossary

chilly: Cool or cold.

perfume: Scented liquid, usually worn on the skin to make it smell pleasant.

swarm: A large number of insects that move as a group.

FINDING WORDS THAT TELL FEELINGS

What do all the words in this word bank have in common?

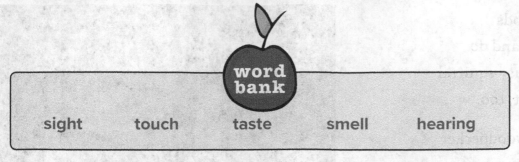

word bank				
sight	touch	taste	smell	hearing

They are the five **senses**! One way that a writer can help the reader feel like they are inside a poem or a story is by using words that remind the reader of the five senses.

Use "A Walk in the Woods" to answer the following questions.

1. Draw a line to match each sensory word with the sense that it reminds you of:

    A. Sight   1. Sweet

    B. Taste   2. Slimy

    C. Hearing   3. Perfume

    D. Smell   4. Yellow

    E. Touch   5. Tapping

2. Which sense would you use to **spot** a busy squirrel?

    A. Touch   B. Hearing   C. Sight

3. Which sense would let you know that something is **chilly**?

    A. Smell   B. Touch   C. Taste

4. Is the *grand perfume* at the end of the poem *really* perfume? Explain why or why not.

    _____

    _____

WHAT KIND OF SENTENCE IS IT?

For a sentence to be a complete sentence, it must have a **punctuation mark** at the end. There are three kinds of end punctuation marks:

.	A **period** is used at the end of **declarative** (telling) sentences that *give information*.
?	A **question mark** is used at the end of **interrogative** sentences that *ask a question*.
!	An **exclamation mark** is used at the end of two kinds of sentences: **exclamatory** sentences that show excitement and feeling, and **imperative** (command) sentences that tell someone what to do.

Activity 1

For each sentence below, circle the kind of sentence that is being shown:

1. Have you ever been on a walk in the woods?

   A. Declarative   B. Interrogative   C. Exclamatory

2. Don't go near that skunk!

   A. Interrogative   B. Exclamatory   C. Imperative

3. I just saw a whole swarm of angry bees!

   A. Exclamatory   B. Imperative   C. Declarative

4. Yesterday, I went on a walk.

   A. Imperative   B. Declarative   C. Interrogative

Activity 2

Place a (? . or !) at the end of each sentence.

1. Will you come to the park with me   2. Watch out for the bees

3. My mom loves the rain   4. Have you ever seen a skunk

Reading and Writing: Literature

TYPES OF WRITING

Two main kinds of writing are **fiction** and **nonfiction**. Fiction is made up and tells a story. Nonfiction gives facts and information. It is not made up.

Page 107 shows text taken from two different pieces of writing. Both pieces of writing are about taking a walk in the woods:

1. Which book gives information?

   _____

2. Which book tells a story?

   _____

3. How do you know?

   _____

4. Draw lines to match the name of each piece of writing with the kind of writing that it is.

   A. "A Walk in the Woods"   1. Nonfiction

   B. "My Class Journal"   2. Fiction

   C. "A Squirrel's Story"   3. Poetry

My Class Journal

Today my class went for a walk. We walked in the woods behind the school. I picked a yellow flower. I learned that you can't see all of a flower, because the roots are under the ground. You can only see the stem, the leaves, and the petals. Next time I pick a flower, I will pull the roots up too.

My friend Alex saw a bird nest. It was on the ground under a tree. It did not have any eggs in it. I wonder what kind of bird built the nest. . .

A Squirrel's Story

One day, Squirrel got tired of picking up seeds and nuts. "I want to eat something else!" she said. She went for a walk to see what she could find. The first thing she saw was a big beehive full of delicious honey.

"Bees," she asked, "Can I please have some of your honey? I am tired of eating seeds and nuts."

The bees laughed. "What would you do with our honey?" they asked.

"You bury your seeds and nuts in the ground for winter. But if you bury honey, it will just get dirt stuck to it!"

"I did not think of that!" Squirrel said. "I will keep looking."

She kept walking until she met a bird. . . "Bird," she asked. "Can I please have some worms with you? I am tired of eating seeds and nuts."

"You do not have a beak like I do. It will be hard for you to pick up the worms out of the dirt."

MAKING DIFFERENT SENTENCES

All sentences must have a **subject** and a **verb**. The subject is who or what the sentence is about, and the verb is the action word that tells what the subject is doing.

> A sentence with just one subject and one verb is a **simple sentence**.
>
> Example: I bought a popsicle. Ali bought an ice cream cone.
>
> When two simple sentences are put together with a **connecting word**, a **compound sentence** is made.
>
> Example: I bought a popsicle and Ali bought an ice cream cone.

Common Connecting Words

for   nor   but   or   so
and   yet

Write an S beside the simple sentences and a C beside the compound sentences.

1. I went for a walk but it started to rain. _____

2. I like to go to the park. _____

3. I saw a squirrel and he was eating a nut. _____

4. Honey is sweet. _____

SPELLING WORDS

Use your knowledge of common spelling patterns to fill in the missing words. Use the picture clues to help you.

Today was a good day for a walk. The _____ was out. There was

not even one cloud in the sky! I took my pet _____ Bruno with me.

I walked on a path, but Bruno wanted to run in the _____.

When we got hot, we stopped to rest under a shady _____. Bruno

even went to _____! When I woke him up, we went home. I

think we will take another walk tomorrow!

SUFFIXES

You can change the meaning of a word by adding different parts to its ending or beginning. When suffixes are added to the end of words, the meaning of the word changes.

> The suffixes **–er**, **-or**, and **–ist** refer to a person who does something.
>
> ## Example:
>
> Paint**er**   A painter is a person who paints.
>
> Visit**or**   A person who visits a place such as a farm or museum.
>
> Art**ist**   A person who makes artwork.

Unscramble the words below to complete the activity. Write the word on the line. Underline the suffix in the word.

1. This person likes to ride in a boat. _____

   r a i l s o

2. This person likes to ride a bicycle. _____

   c s t c y l i

3. This person is very good at dancing. _____

   e c d r a n

WRITE YOUR NARRATIVE

A good story has three parts: the ***characters, setting,*** and ***plot***. These are called the elements of a story. The writer of a story can use these story elements to describe actions, thoughts, and feelings. The plot of a narrative story tells what happens in the story. The conclusion of the story is the ending that summarizes what you wrote about.

Imagine that you are an animal that lives in the woods. Write a story about what happens when you see a person for the first time ever! Make sure that your story has characters, a setting, a plot, and a conclusion. Use the graphic organizer to plan the elements for your story.

Characters	Setting	Plot
Who is your story about?	**Where** does your story take place?	**What** takes place?

WRITE YOUR NARRATIVE

Use this graphic organizer to plan your story.

What happens first . . .

Next . . .

Then . . .

Finally, how does your story end?

Use your outline from page 112 to develop your story below. Plan an introduction, a body, and a conclusion.

Introduction (Set up your story. Who is in it? Where and when is it set?):

_____

_____

_____

_____

_____

Body (Describe what happens in your story):

_____

_____

_____

_____

_____

Conclusion (How does your story end?):

_____

_____

_____

_____

_____

REVIEW

Congratulations! You have completed the lessons in this section. Now you will have the opportunity to practice some of the skills you just learned.

Reading Fluency

Adults: Time your student reading aloud for one minute. Make a note of where your student is at the end of one minute. (Your student should be able to read 10–60 words per minute.) Have your student continue reading to the end of the text to answer the questions that follow.

The Camel and the Pig

An Indian Folktale

One day, Camel and Pig made a bet. Camel felt that it was better to be	16
tall. But Pig thought it was better to be short. If Camel was right, he would	32
have to give Pig his hump. But if Pig was right, then he would have to give	49
Camel his snout.	52
They found a garden with a low wall. Camel reached his long neck over	66
the top. While Camel was busy eating, Pig just watched. He was too short	80
to even see the plants in the garden. "Don't you wish you were tall like me?"	96
said Camel.	98
Later they found another garden. This garden had a tall wall all around	111
it. There was a hole in the gate on one side of the wall. Pig walked through	128
the hole and started eating. However, Camel was too tall. He could not get in.	143
The wall was even too high for him reach over. "Now I bet you wish that	159
you were short like me!" laughed Pig.	166
Camel and Pig thought about their bet.	173
"Maybe you should keep your hump," Pig said.	181
"And maybe you should keep your snout," Camel said.	190
"In the end," they said together, "sometimes being tall is better, and	202
sometimes being short is better. Neither one is best!"	211

Words read in 1 minute — errors = WPM

Activity 1

Use what you know about prepositions to circle the preposition in each sentence below:

1. The camel stood outside the garden.

2. He reached over the wall.

3. The pig walked through the gate.

4. He ate the plants in the garden.

Activity 2

Use what you know about punctuation to add a punctuation mark to the end of each sentence:

1. Wow, I got to ride on a camel today

2. Pigs are shorter than camels

3. Would you like to be short

4. Let me in the garden right now

Activity 3

Use the information in the box and what you already know about word endings and beginnings to fill in the blank in each sentence.

The ending –er has two meanings. It can mean **more** or **a person who does something.**

Example: Sam is **taller** (more tall) than his brother.

The **teacher** (person who teaches) read a story to the class.

The beginning re– means **again**.

Example: I had to **reapply** (apply again) my sunscreen after I went swimming.

1. The camel's neck is _____ (more long) than the pig's neck.

2. The pig and the camel had to _____ (consider again) their bet when they discovered that neither tall nor short was better.

3. The _____ (person who gardens) was not happy when he saw the pig in his garden.

4. He had to _____ (plant again) some of his vegetables.

Activity 4

Circle the meaning of –er that is being used in each word.

1. Builder (more/person who)

2. Louder (more/person who)

3. Eater (more/person who)

Activity 5

Use what you know about words with meanings that are similar, but not the same, to answer the following questions:

1. The owner of the garden yelled, screamed, and stomped his feet when he saw the pig eating his vegetables. He chased the pig away and told him never to come back. He was _____.

    A. Upset   B. Angry   C. Furious

2. Carrots are the pig's favorite vegetable. He eats some every day. The pig _____ carrots.

    A. Likes   B. Loves   C. Worships

3. The camel wants to throw some fruit to the pig on the other side of the wall. He knows that he needs to be gentle so he does not hurt the pig or bruise the fruit. He should _____ the fruit.

    A. Toss   B. Pitch   C. Hurl

4. The pig had to _____ so that the camel could hear him on the other side of the wall.

    A. Talk   B. Yell   C. Whisper

Activity 6

Use what you know about words to circle the conjunction word in each sentence.

1. The gardener planted lettuce and his neighbor planted apples.

2. The pig thought it was better to be short until he was too short to reach the food.

3. The camel could not get through the gate in the wall because he was too tall.

4. After they ended their bet, the camel and the pig became good friends.

UNDERSTAND

Now let's review and practice the reading skills that you have learned.

Little Red Hen

One day Little Red Hen found a grain of wheat lying on the ground.

"Who will plant this?" she asked.

"Not I," said the cat.

"Not I," said the goose.

"Not I," said the rat.

"Then I will," said Little Red Hen. So she buried the grain in the rich brown dirt. After a while it grew up yellow and **ripe**.

"The wheat is ripe now," said Little Red Hen.

"Who will cut and **thresh** it?"

"Not I," said the cat.

"Not I," said the goose.

"Not I," said the rat.

"Then I will," said Little Red Hen. So she cut it with her sharp bill and threshed it with her wings.

Then she asked, "Who will take this wheat to the **mill**?"

"Not I," said the cat.

"Not I," said the goose.

"Not I," said the rat.

"Then I will," said Little Red Hen. So she took the wheat to the mill, where it was ground into fine white flour. Then she carried the flour home.

"Who will make me some bread with this flour?" she asked.

"Not I," said the cat.

"Not I," said the goose.

"Not I," said the rat.

"Then I will," sighed Little Red Hen. So she made and baked the bread.

When the bread was finished baking a delicious scent filled the air.

Then she said, "Now we shall see who will eat this bread."

"We will! We will!" said the cat, the goose, and the rat.

"I am quite sure you would," laughed Little Red Hen, "if you could get it!"

Then she called her chicks, and they ate up all the bread. There was none left at all for the cat, or the goose, or the rat.

glossary

mill: A building with a machine that crushes or grinds things, for example, grain into flour.

ripe: Finished growing and ready to pick and eat.

thresh: To separate the grain from the rest of the plant, usually by beating it.

Activity 1

Use "Little Red Hen" to answer the following questions.

1. Who is the main character? _____

2. Which event is from the **middle** of the story?
   A. Little Red Hen goes to the mill
   B. Little Red Hen calls her chicks
   C. Little Red Hen finds a grain

3. What is one **problem** Little Red Hen has in the story? _____

_____

4. How does she solve, or fix, the problem? _____

    _____

5. What is the **moral**, or lesson, of the story?
    A. Sharing is always the right thing to do.
    B. Family will help you even when friends will not.
    C. If you are not willing to work, you will not get the reward.

6. What does the bolded word tell you about how Little Red Hen feels?

    "Then I will," **sighed** Little Red Hen.

    _____

7. Match each sensing word from the story to the sense it reminds you of.

    A. Brown   1. Taste

    B. Scent   2. Sight

    C. Called   3. Touch

    D. Delicious   4. Smell

    E. Sharp   5. Hearing

8. Find another sensory word in the story and record it in the space below:
    Sensory words: _____ Senses it reminds me of: _____

9. Who is the **narrator** of the story?
    A. Little Red Hen   B. The author   C. The cat

10. Which part of the story does this **illustration** show?
    A. Beginning   B. Middle   C. End

11. What happens after the part of the story in the illustration?

    A. Little Red Hen's chicks eat the bread.

    B. Little Red Hen eats the bread all by herself.

    C. Little Red Hen shares the bread with the cat, goose, and rat.

DISCOVER

Write Your Explanation

An explanation is written to explain how or why something happens. A good explanation should have an introduction, or beginning, that grabs the reader's attention. It should also have plenty of facts and details that support the main idea, or topic, of the explanation. A conclusion, or ending, is used to complete the explanation of the topic.

In the story "Little Red Hen," you learned some of the things that must happen in order to make a loaf of bread. Now it's your turn! In this section, you will be writing an explanation of how to make one of your favorite foods.

Use the organizer to plan your writing:

The food I want to write about is:

Step 1:

Step 2:

Step 3:

Step 4:

Conclusion:

Use your outline from page 124 to develop your work below. Plan an introduction, a body with your steps, and a conclusion.

Introduction (Topic sentence that states the main idea):

_____

_____

_____

_____

Body (Include details that support the main idea):

_____

_____

_____

_____

_____

Conclusion (Concluding sentences that summarize the main idea):

_____

_____

_____

_____

_____

My Journal

_____

_____

_____

_____

_____

_____

_____

_____

_____

_____

_____

_____

_____

_____

_____

_____

_____

_____

_____

_____

My Journal

Answer Key

Reading Foundational Skills

Unit 1 – Phonics

Lesson 1 – Learning Short and Long Vowel Sounds
Page 4. 1. B; 2. A

Lesson 2 – Consonant Blends
Page 6. 1. A. bl; B. gl; C. dr; 2. A

Lesson 3 – Word Parts
Page 8. 1. A; 2. C

Lesson 4 – Understanding Word Sounds
Page 9. A. k/i/s; B. p/a/k; C. s/e/m; Challenge: A

Unit 2 – Phonics and Word Recognition

Lesson 1 – Understanding Digraphs
Page 12. 1. A. sh; B. wh; C. ng; Challenge: B

Lesson 2 – Spelling Regular Words
Page 13. Activity 1: Answers will vary. Sample answers: fit, hit, bit, kit, pit, sit

Page 14. Activity 2: Answers will vary. Sample answers: pat, pet, pit, pot, put

Lesson 3 – The Silent "–e"
Page 15. 1. e; 2. yes; 3. long

Lesson 4 – Vowel Teams
Page 16. 1. C; 2. B; 3. A; Challenge: boot, boat

Lesson 5 – Vowels in Syllables
Page 17. Activity 1: Circle: someone, peanut; A. some | one; B. pea | nut; C. goat; Activity 2: A. 2 syllables; B. 3 syllables; C. 1 syllable

Lesson 6 – Understanding Two-Syllable Words
Page 19. Activity 1: A. un/der; B. o/pen; C. an/swer; Circle: open

Page 20. Activity 2: A. fun/ny, 2; B. let/ter, 2; C. yel/low, 2

Lesson 7 – Changing Nouns by Their Endings
Page 22. 1. boxes; 2. cats; 3. kisses

Lesson 8 – Changing Verbs by Their Endings
Page 22. Activity 1: 1. plays; 2. washes; 3. buzzing

Page 23. Activity 2: 1. baked; 2. jumped

Lesson 9 – Reading Irregular Words
Page 24. Activity 1: A. What; B. laughed; C. knock; Activity 2: 1. C; 2. A; 3. B

Page 25. Challenge: night, through, once, laugh, know

Unit 3 – Fluency: Read with Purpose and Understanding

Lesson 1 – Thank You, Mrs. Spot!
Page 29. Guided Questions: 1. cook, share; 2. The kids like Mrs. Spot and are thankful for the food she gives them. 3. Answers will vary. Any picture of a gift for Mrs. Spot is sufficient.

Lesson 2 – A Bee Tale
Page 31. Guided Questions: 1. Bees give pollen to the crops and fruits; 2. Oranges, apples, pears, and limes; 3. Answers will vary. Any image of a bee on a flower or crop is sufficient.

Reading and Writing: Informational Texts

Unit 4 – Maps and Globes

Lesson 1 – How to Use Maps and Globes
Page 36. Finding the Main Idea and Key Details: 1. B

Page 37. 2. C; 3. B; 4. Answers will vary. Sample answer: A map is a tool you use to find directions. A globe is a ball-shaped model of the Earth showing continents, countries, and oceans. 5.

Page 38. Connecting Ideas: 1. C; 2. A; 3. C

Page 39. Pictures Help Explain a Text: Activity 1: 1. South; 2. North and East

Page 40. Activity 2: 1. Map; 2. Globe; 3. Map; 4. Map; 5. Globe; 6. Map

Page 41. Compare Illustrations and Text: 1. P; 2. T; 3. T; 4. T; 5. T

Page 42. Using Adjectives: 1. small; 2. blue; 3. bad; 4. many; 5. good; Activity 2: 1. round; 2. soggy; 3. helpful

Page 43. Using Commas: 1. December 31, 2024; 2. July 18, 2021; 3. I am going to the zoo, park, café, and library; Activity 2: B; Activity 3: C

Page 44. Activity 4: 1. August 8, 2025; 2. They like dolls, cats, and pink things.

Page 45. Using Root Words: 1. sleep; 2. bus; 3. small; 4. look; 5. walk; 6. eat; 7. talk; 8. draw; Real-Life Connections: Activity 1: Answers will vary. Sample answer: My family and I went to Silver Dollar City. We used the park map to find the location of the roller coaster, Fire in the Hole.

Page 46. Activity 2: Answers will vary. Sample answer: Nice Elephants Should Wave; Activity 3: Answers will vary. Sample answer: A mapmaker needs to be a good artist and be able to draw. They also need to be good at math and geography.

Unit 5 – Amazing Animals

Lesson 1 – Dolphin Diaries

Page 50. Finding the Main Idea and Details: Answers will vary. Sample answer: Dolphins and humans do many of the same things. Dolphins help each other eat. Dolphins communicate with their pod. Dolphins snuggle close to their pod.

Page 52. Understanding Verbs: Activity 1: 1. used; 2. learned; 3. helped; 4. showed; 5. talked; Activity 2: 1. past; 2. present; 3. past; 4. future

Page 53. Using End Punctuation: 1. I went swimming yesterday. 2. Did you see the dolphin show? 3. Watch out, the dolphin is splashing water!

Page 54. Challenge: Answers will vary. Sample answers: My mom took me to Florida to see the dolphins. How do dolphins learn to do tricks? Wow, dolphins are amazing!

Page 55. Using Diagrams: 1. head

Page 56. 2. pectoral fins; 3. tail

Lesson 2 – An Elephant Essay

Page 58. Understanding Text Features: 1. An Elephant Essay; 2. C; 3. C

Page 59. Comparing Different Types of Information: Answers will vary. Sample answers: Elephants are tame, friendly with people, used in tourism; 2. B

Page 60. 3. A

Page 61. Comparing and Contrasting Articles: Answers will vary. Sample answers: Similar (stays with their group; eats a lot; uses rostrum/trunk similarly); Different (dolphins live in water/elephants live on land; dolphin eats fish/elephant eats plants; dolphin can hold breath for 30 minutes/elephants use trunk to take a shower)

Page 62. Comparing Characteristics

Dolphins	Elephants	Both
Rostrum	Trunk	Eats a lot
Holds breath	Eats plants	Stays with group
Fluke	Drinks 50 gallons of water	Shows love
Swims	Can pick up marbles	Communicates

Stop and Think! Units 4–5 Review

Page 67. Activity 1: 1. used; 2. makes; 3. will talk; Activity 2: Answers 1–3 will vary. Sample answers: 1. blue; 2. cute; 3. Fast; Activity 3: 1. The scientist wants to talk to dolphins.; 2.Did you hear the dolphin noises?; 3. Dolphins are amazing!

Page 68. Activity 4: 1. watch, watched; 2. look, looked; 3. help, helped; Activity 5: Elephants – mammal, breathe air, live on land, eat plants. Dolphin – mammal, breathe air, fins, eats fish. Human – mammal, breathe air, hair, lives on land, eats fish and plants

Stop and Think! Units 4–5 Understand

Page 71. Activity 1: 1. An Artist Named Ruby. 2. A canvas is a white board that artists paint on. It is important to Ruby's story because she paints on one. 3. The colors Ruby uses in the painting and the way it looks. 4. Both animals are important because they help animals and humans communicate and get along.

Page 72. Activity 2: Answers will vary. Sample answers: "An Elephant Essay" and "An Artist Named Ruby" are similar because they both are about elephants. They both show how elephants are like humans. They also both show how elephants can do things that people cannot.

Reading and Writing: Literature

Unit 6 – Folktales

Lesson 1 – The Story of the Three Bears

Page 81. Characters, Settings, and Events: 1. B; 2. Answers will vary. Sample answers: The porridge is too hot to eat. Goldilocks is sleeping in one of their beds. 3. Goldilocks has very bad manners.

Page 82. 4. Top left–4, Top right–1, Bottom left–2, Bottom right–3; Who Is Telling the Story? 1. C; 2. Answers may vary. Sample answer: Students may say that the author uses large, medium, and small print to match the size of the bear speaking.

Answer Key

Page 83. Spelling: 1. hair; 2. door; 3. spoon; 4. sad

Lesson 2 – Scrapefoot

Page 86. Who Is Telling the Story? 1. A; 2. Answers will vary. Sample answer: The author uses words like "said" to signal when characters are talking, uses quotation marks, or in this instance uses all capital letters or italicized type; 3. A; 4. Answers will vary. Sample answers: Students may use any of the little bear's three lines, which appear in italics in the text. Comparing and Contrasting Stories: 1. C

Page 87. Answers may vary. Sample answers: In both "Scrapefoot" and "The Story of the Three Bears," both Goldilocks and Scrapefoot walked into the bears' house. They both tried out the chairs, food, and beds. They are different because Scrapefoot is a wolf and Goldilocks is a girl. Scrapefoot tried milk, Goldilocks tried the porridge. The bears threw Scrapefoot out the window and Goldilocks jumped out of the window and ran away.

Page 88. Using Determiners: the, a, This, a, These, the, Those, that

Page 89. Understanding the Clues: 1. Comfortable means feeling happy and relaxed; 2. Thirsty means having an uncomfortable feeling because you need something to drink; 3. Something that tastes bitter and unpleasant like a lemon; 4. Feeling very afraid.

Unit 7 – Messages and Morals

Lesson 1 – The Happy Prince

Page 94. Finding the Central Message and Key Details: 1. The Happy Prince and the swallow; 2. B; 3. To help the prince by staying with him and being his eyes; 4. C; 5. A: 2, B: 3, C: 1

Page 95. 6. A; 7. B. Words that Tell About Feelings: 1. Answers may vary. Sample answer: The Happy Prince is sad or not really happy; 2. B; 3. C; 4. sad

Page 96. Pictures Help with Understanding: 1. A; 2. Sapphires—Answers will vary. Sample answer: The picture matches the definition of a sapphire in the word bank, or the picture resembles the prince's eye as shown in the illustration; 3. B

Page 97. Using Prepositions: 1. on; 2. from, to; 3. with; 4. around; Punctuating Sentences: 1. ?; 2. .; 3. ?; 4. !; 5. !; 6. .

Page 98. Prefixes: Activity 1: 1. unhappy; 2. impossible; 3. unfair; 4. unable

Page 99. Using Conjunctions: 1. but; 2. after; 3. so; 4. yet; Challenge: Answers will vary. Sample answer: I like the water, but I haven't learned to swim.

Unit 8 – Poetry

Lesson 1 – A Walk in the Woods

Page 104. Finding Words that Tell Feelings: 1. A: 4, B: 1, C: 5, D: 3, E: 2; 2. C; 3. B; 4. Answers will vary. Sample answer: The "perfume" is actually the smell of a skunk and note that the writer of the poem is adding humor by calling something that stinks "perfume," a term usually used for things that smell good.

Page 105. What Kind of Sentence Is It? Activity 1: 1. B; 2. C; 3. A; 4. B. Activity 2: 1. ?; 2. !; 3. .; 4. ?

Page 106. Types of Writing: 1. Answers may vary. Sample answer: "My Class Journal" is describing something that really happened and gives information about flowers; 2. "A Squirrel's Story." 3. Answers will vary. Sample answer: "A Squirrel's Story" has made up animal characters and tells the things that they do and say; 3. Answers will vary; 4. A: 3, B: 1, C: 2

Page 108. Making Different Sentences: Activity 1: 1. C; 2. S; 3. C; 4. S

Page 109. Spelling Words: sun, dog, grass, tree, sleep

Page 110. Suffixes: 1. sailor; 2. cyclist; 3. dancer

Stop and Think! Units 6–8 Review

Page 116. Activity 1: 1. outside; 2. over; 3. through; 4. in; Activity 2: 1. !; 2. .; 3. ?; 4. !

Page 117. Activity 3: 1. longer; 2. reconsider; 3. gardener; 4. replant; Activity 4: 1. person who; 2. more; 3. person who

Page 118. Activity 5: 1. C; 2. B; 3. A; 4. B; Activity 6: 1. and; 2. until

Page 119. 3. because; 4. after

Stop and Think! Units 6–8 Understand

Page 121. Activity 1: 1. Little Red Hen; 2. A; 3. Answers will vary. Sample answers: Little Red Hen cannot get any of the other animals to help her plant the wheat, harvest and thresh the wheat, take the wheat to the mill, or bake the bread.

Page 122. 4. Answers will vary. Sample answer: Little Red Hen did all the work herself; 5. C; 6. Answers will vary. Little Red Hen is sad or frustrated that no one will help her, or is tired of having to do everything herself; 7. A: 2, B: 4, C: 5, D: 1, E: 3; 8. Answers will vary. Sample answer: Sensory word: sharp. Sense it reminds me of: touch. Sensory words: delicious scent. Senses it reminds me of: taste and smell. 9. B; 10. C

Page 123. 11. A